THE MALE
IN CRISIS

THE MALE IN CRISIS

Karl Bednarik

Translated from the German by Helen Sebba

ALFRED · A · KNOPF

New York   1970

CONTENTS

PREFACE

This book presents the thesis that in modern industrial society the majority of men suffer from a central disturbance in their masculine, life. I have tried to show that prevailing conditions are introducing radical changes in three of the most vital areas of masculine behavior, changes so crucial that we may well speak of a crisis in masculine life itself. This crisis is treated under three main headings: "The Crisis of Eros," "The Crisis of Activism and Aggression," and "The Crisis of Authority." The book separates these areas for purely methodological reasons; in reality, of course, they are interlinked in an extremely complex way. Their inner connection, as well as the logic of the sequence in which they are discussed, should become evident as the book proceeds.

Chapter 1 presents an overview of what is meant by the crisis of masculinity. I attempt first to show that the frequent predictions concerning the evolution of a new matriarchy rest on false premises and that despite feminine emancipation, it is not woman who constitutes the threat to man. The danger originates within the male world itself, in the male technological machine which permits a few "Big Brothers" to make the vital decisions for more and more people. Through its own social and technological activity, the male world itself has created the conditions that are moving contemporary society toward a superpatriarchy. This means that for the majority of men, the traditional male role is jeopardized; the ordinary male is pushed increasingly into play activity and a female pattern of consumer behavior.

The subdivisions of Chapter 1 present two of the most obvious symptoms of the crisis of masculinity. The first is the impotent anger smoldering beneath the surface of the male world and seeking outlet either in sporadic outbursts of aggression or in the informal but institutionalized discharge rituals of sports or the arts. Here the literature of the "angry young men" is relevant. The second symptom is the absurdist revolt of contemporary youth. The "universal protest" so often encountered today among young people —a protest which threatens to become a revolt in favor of meaninglessness—is a masculine attempt, usually unconscious yet nonetheless defiant, to stake out new territories in a totally managed world and to realize group ideals through new social mobility.

Chapter 2, "The Crisis of Eros," begins with a discussion of the commercialization and consequent inflation of sex. This results in a profound alienation of sexuality, which is wrenched out of its life context and overloaded with importance. The libido is thus divorced from the emotional relationship with the partner and from ethical responsibility—not at all what the advocates of sex reform intended. The channeling of other instinctual drives into the area of sex is of paramount importance. The injection of surplus aggressiveness into sex leads to a false consciousness in the man-woman relationship. The result is a war between the sexes that breeds a latent sadism in society, one symptom of which is sensation-seeking interest in sexual crimes. I try to show that the cult of the young girl in the present male generation actually masks a shying away from the female as an equal, just as currently fashionable homosexuality masks a retreat from masculinity. The flight from the outward world through the increasing use of drugs is also discussed in this context, as are the very real sexual difficulties of adolescents which result from precocious sexualization. The core of the second chapter deals with the progressive transformation of the *complementary* sexual relationship between men and women (acceptance of the opposite as a harmonious supplement to the self) into a *reciprocal* relationship (an exchange of equivalents, through which love can become a kind of merchandise). This change, together with the practical effects of reliable methods of contraception, produces a new situation in which the male can easily be overtaxed erotically; the active sexual role then passes to the woman. The sexual act becomes competitive and subject to the tyranny of the orgasm. In brief, sexuality needs to be liberated from the commercial orientation into which it has been manipulated; the problems of the contemporary Eros originate elsewhere—namely, in frustrated masculine activism and authority.

Chapter 3 takes up "The Crisis of Activism and Aggression." Behaviorist psychology has recognized aggressive masculine behavior as a biological necessity—curiously enough, at precisely that point in history when aggression in the social and political sphere must be censured because the development of armaments has carried it to absurdity, and at the point when changes in the social structures of our time have altered moral values so that aggression seems no longer justifiable. I show that the legitimate militant behavior by the male which was encouraged from earliest times has now become almost impossible. Technological progress has upset the ancient notion of heroism. The military leader of men becomes a battlefield bureaucrat, and the real purpose of wars—namely, safeguarding the civilian population's existence—is no longer fulfilled.

Technological progress causes equally serious conflicts in the male's working life. Human independence is disappearing to an ever-increasing extent, for all the small forms of social organization are being absorbed into industrial and bureaucratic superstructures. Specialization and functionalization of work are making it increasingly difficult for the individual to attain full humanity. A typical symptom is the growth of a sociologically almost indefinable group, the white-collar workers, whose "unity" is maintained purely to camouflage a new elite of top-ranking bureaucrats. In present conditions this elite deprives the majority of all opportunity for a freely developing activism. Yet the male is by nature active; even his aggressive instinct is an expression of this facet of his being. What is now to become of his frustrated activism?

Chapter 4, "The Crisis of Authority," suggests a means of resolving the crisis of masculinity. It points out that the growth of social superstructures causes anonymous bureaucratic authorities to encroach more and more upon the individual's domain of authority, especially the father's authority within the family. Yet only within this specific area, the area where masculine authority asserts itself, can the problem actually be solved through a process of restructuring society and democratizing authority. Fortunately, in addition to the tendencies toward elaboration of the superstructure, trends toward fundamental democratization and group activity are also making themselves felt. I have tried to show that these tendencies must be supported and reinforced if we hope to avoid social catastrophe. Unless man is willing to be feminized, he must bring about a new distribution of authority in society; he must learn to exert the democratic responsibility due him as a mature man. Only then will he be ready to assume moral responsibility for solving the problems of Eros and aggressiveness in the world of today.

THE MALE IN CRISIS

1

THE MALE IN CRISIS

"Every man is the son of his actions."
Cervantes in *Don Quixote*

The male in crisis? Why not *man* in crisis—or, for that matter, woman in crisis? Because men are more acutely affected than women by the changes, upheavals, and revolutions of our time: because it is men who have brought these about and who continue to bring them about. Men, not women, have shaped the course of history. Women may set the tone in "society," but in Society it is set by men. From the smallest bodies and associations up to the great government organizations and international superstructures, it is men who bear the responsibility. They supply the rulers, popes, high priests, grand masters, prophets and founders of religions, tyrants, philosophers, speculative thinkers, researchers, and discoverers. With very few exceptions it has been men who have laid the scientific groundwork for changes in our reality; they are responsible for the development of industrial technology and the organization of productive labor.

3

The male has always been the inventor of mankind's future, the stage director of history. Armaments and weapons down to the atom bomb have been the work of male smiths, artists, inventors, warriors, scientists. But even pacifist movements against war and militarism have commonly been led by men. For organized pacifism is a form of social warfare or political action aiming to educate society and change the conditions of life, and apart from a few exceptional women this kind of warfare is also a masculine preserve.

It should not be necessary to say that this is no diatribe against women; nor does the fear of an imminent matriarchy prompt this delineation of a male crisis. Despite the political and economic emancipation of women, there is not really a social trend toward a matriarchal form of government—which in any case is not synonymous with rule by women. A matriarchy is rather a kind of "rule by uncles," in which succession is through the mother but the decisions are made by her brothers. Thus in a matriarchal order every father is head not of his own but of his sister's family. This is obviously not the case in our society. But neither does our society show much evidence of matriarchal authority—that is to say, of mother-dominated families. In the few cases which do appear, it would have to be determined whether the woman has deliberately "seized" authority or has simply been forced to assume it as a result of the husband's absence, weakness, or incapacity. Often it will turn out that the woman is exercising authority only reluctantly. Judged by our standards of emancipation from conventional ties, particularly the emancipation of children and young people, the woman with several children belongs to one of the most enslaved categories of humanity in existence. Despite some appearances of authority and freedom of movement, woman's position at home, in industry, in the government bureaucracy, and in politics is commonly a subordinate or menial one. She usually does the least prestigious work and does it for lower pay than men in comparable positions. Hence the warnings of a coming matriarchy seem without foundation. This is not to say that woman is a second-class or inferior being; the temptation is rather to see her as a higher, or at any rate, a better one. In any case, she differs radically from the male, in body, in mind, in life aims, and in basic interests.

Certainly it is not a matter of his pride in belonging to the chosen sex which has caused the male to make and to continue making his achievements. The literature of social criticism is full of dire predictions concerning the bomb and the pill, those two artifacts let loose on a world of controlled mass media, expanding bureaucracies, population and knowledge explosions, pollution, famine, revolutions, and wars. Responsibility for this state of affairs lies with men—discoverers, producers, researchers, and organizers. Even most of the great crimes have been committed by men: there are no female counterparts of Al Capone, Beria, Himmler, Jack the Ripper, and Landru.

The crisis under consideration is undoubtedly being experienced by the human race in general, but it is the human male who has brought it upon mankind, beginning with himself. Woman may share the blame, but she is not as directly responsible. Both the bomb and the pill were invented by men. Both, in their different ways, have drastically transformed man's consciousness; yet of the two, the pill may turn out to have the more devastating effect upon the male consciousness as such. The pill undeniably makes woman less of a woman, in that sex can now be for her what it has hitherto been only for the male: a form of play, a pleasure to be pursued without fear of practical consequences. Nevertheless, she can still choose—as long as the pill is not universally administered to whole populations by decree—whether to be so emancipated or not. But what about the man, freed from his traditional obligation to take responsibility for begetting children? His virility loses a certain ethical attribute derived from its biological effect. Sexually, as woman's scope is broadened, his is diminished; he ceases to be the initiator, relinquishes his sexual "superiority." The decision whether or not to "make" a child passes from the man to the woman, and again he loses something of the male quality as the "doer," not because of the woman's initiative, but in consequence of his own scientific discoveries and technological capacity.

Since it is the male who takes action and who keeps changing the world, including himself, the so-called emancipation of woman is also directly or indirectly the result of masculine efforts which have produced changes so fundamental as to make woman's emancipation possible. It is the same man-made changes which are now so deeply disrupting the life of the male. For they enable a constantly diminishing number of men, an elite of "Big Brothers," to monopolize the traditional male powers of decision and action, leaving the great majority of males psychologically deprived, curtailed in their freedom and their expansionist drive to action, and under such moral and practical pressures that one is justified in speaking of the emasculation of our era.

The male is obviously in retreat, though not from the onslaught of emancipated woman or any "coming matriarchy." He is in retreat from what he himself has wrought, from a world of overautomatized, overcentralized controls that make him feel superfluous as a man. The dread of a coming matriarchy does not reflect a genuine threat arising from such a development in society; it is merely the symptom of the feminized state of much of the contemporary male world. No man who feels secure in his masculinity spontaneously fears the competition of woman; he knows that her role in life is fundamentally different from his own. Only a man who has been in one way or another shorn of his male self-confidence can regard woman as a competitor. And it is only since the industrial revolution and the progressive perfection of industrialization to the point of electronic automation that the specifically masculine self-image has become profoundly disturbed. To be a man, in the traditional sense, has become increasingly more difficult in the technologically advanced, white-dominated civilizations we are talking about.

This is not to lament the fact that woman has begun to play a greater role in public life than she has ever played before, nor to demand that she withdraw from the position she has won. On the contrary, I am much in favor of her participating still more fully and directly in the shaping of modern civilization. I have no interest in retaining the old sexual norms, shored up by religion and metaphysics, which say that woman is "subject" to man and must obey him unconditionally. But the indisputable fact is that women are less well qualified for some activities and better qualified for others, that they are not qualified at all for some tasks and exclusively qualified for others. So if they enjoy it, by all means let women engage in politics, govern countries, climb the Himalayas, have themselves shot into space, study physics, direct industries, go in for ski jumping, race automobiles, or do anything else they choose. They will soon discover which things they can do well. I doubt, however—and this is probably the crucial point—that they are particularly happy when they are competing with men.

In politics, for example, women are more dependent on men than men on women. With few exceptions their status, like that of Mrs. Roosevelt, Comrade Furtseva, Mme de Gaulle, and Lady Churchill, is conferred by men, and they accommodate themselves to men more than men do to women. It would be hard to find a case of three brothers adapting such radically different spheres of life as the three Chinese Sung sisters, of whom the first was married to Sun Yat-sen, the second to Chiang Kai-shek, and the third to an American millionaire.

As for the military professions, no army in the world has yet had a female general staff. And if such a thing should

ever happen, the women would merely be venturing into a
field created by men. Today the male world goes so far as
to use women as military auxiliaries and to tell them that this
means true freedom, true emancipation—striking evidence
that it is the male himself who is the problem. Woman's
share in the decisions is a pious democratic self-deception.
Wherever she has any real say, she has subordinated herself
to man and his strivings.

What is actually happening in this phenomenon called
the emancipation of women? In the male consciousness the
pill is finally making woman his plaything, even though she
may not see herself in this light and may even believe that
the pill can help her achieve true freedom. This of course
aggravates the self-disruption of the masculine consciousness, for in the process man too becomes increasingly his own
plaything. In our time the concept of the playboy has
emerged to become a formative image all over the world, an
image symptomatic of a climate in which many men are
drawing farther and farther away from the traditional masculine role that has up to now been taken as an expression
of "the true nature of man." Although a partnership in play
may seem attractive at first because it is free of all animal—
that is to say, biological—seriousness, it undeniably disturbs
and invalidates something of the primordial interchange between the sexes. Mutual adjustment and reciprocal responsibility are lost. Ultimately the woman is the loser, since as
we all know, interest in playthings does not last very long;
toys are most interesting when they are not easy to get.

What does the male do in this situation? He turns to

other things: cars, drugs, ideas, causes, and wars. And woman, for fear of losing him, must follow him into male territory, where she is likely to be and feel inferior to him. Today she can even go to war—certainly the most perfidious idea men ever thought up. We are tempted to believe that only sadistic rapist-killers or woman-hating homosexual generals could be behind such a measure, and that established male society in general is beginning to lose interest in woman *qua* woman—or has already substantially lost it. This is true at least of the leaders and the male groups responsible for such circumstances. A society which tolerates conditions in which individual men no longer defend and protect women must be regarded as considerably emasculated.

The male world has maneuvered itself into this fix by creating political, economic, scientific, and technological institutions that bring a few men to the top, to usurp all powers of decision and action from the majority. These few are not necessarily great men; they are more often highly adaptable careerists, "operators," "organization men." The effect of their dominance, however, is to infantilize or feminize the male population in general, which acquiesces in surrendering independence for a promise of security—a security which may turn out to be the greatest illusion of all. In a world dependent upon expensive technotronic gadgets and weapons, ruled by gigantic private and public bureaucracies, the majority of men are learning to capitulate as males, inasmuch as the traditional male roles have lost validity for them.

What is meant here by the male role is the cultural stylization of the man's function in society as generally conceived. Whether this cultural stylization and the norms for masculine life derived from it can be scientifically proved to have their roots in the "nature of man" is by no means sure. On the contrary, most representatives of the modern sciences of man, particularly psychology and sociology, believe that cultural stylizations are fairly dominant, while man's nature is unstable and changeable. Other scientists, however—chiefly behavioralists, comparative anthropologists, and biologists—consider certain forms of instinct fixation in man to be not only plausible but unquestionable. Here one opinion carries as much weight as another; the case for both sides is open to attack. On the whole it seems to be agreed that man possesses only weak, vestigial instincts which can readily be influenced by reflection, consciousness, and rationality; that human behavior is not imprinted as a pattern, but that behavior patterns are largely imparted by learning processes, unconscious and conscious. It is admittedly difficult to believe that throughout history the male role has been based on cultural stylization alone—that there is no such thing as "the nature of man," and hence that male and female modes of behavior are not unmistakably differentiated by any naturally fixed characteristics. At any rate, even if the differences in the two sexes' modes of behavior really represent nothing but cultural stylization, they have produced remarkably distinctive behavior profiles. Whatever the reasons, the decisive fact is that the male's self-understanding in the world up to now has led to the clear-cut sexual differentiation of performance which has survived for so long.

In my opinion, however, certain specific needs and

qualities in the male sex seem to match this characteristic profile of the male role. Without doubt vast differences exist between men of different races, peoples, and nations, as well as within these peoples and races themselves. We do not need comparative ethnology to tell us that the world includes six-foot giants with bulging muscles and tiny, delicate pygmies with narrow hands; it contains aggressive bullies as well as charming, fawning flatterers. Yet often the weaklings are the ones who go in for the most risky work, while athletic types are occasionally to be found changing diapers and washing dishes. In every age some men must have found it hard to adjust to the culturally given male role. We can assume, however, that on the whole the distinctly masculine character of this role was agreed upon by the majority; otherwise it could not have survived for so long. There must be something in masculine nature that permits and encourages cultural stylizations of this kind, and whatever it is must be inherent in the weakest and gentlest of men too.

As Helmut Schelsky has shown, the difference between men and women can no longer be formulated in terms like these: "Directly or indirectly men show a stronger will to have things their own way and greater aggressiveness; they are more daring and fearless and rougher in manners, language, and feelings. Women are compassionate and more sympathetic, more timid, more sensitive esthetically, generally more emotional (or at least more demonstrative), more moralistic, although they show less emotional self-control."[1] Another of these false ideas about the male role is that men are not vain: in fact, men are no less vain than women; their vanity merely takes a different form. Equally misleading rules of conduct derived from an idealized version of the male role are expressed in clichés such as "Men don't cry" and "Men don't gossip."

Yet the weaknesses of such formulations do not justify the conclusion that there are no fundamental differences between masculine and feminine life styles. Men have tear glands and wagging tongues and use them, though perhaps differently from women, with different motives and different sensibilities. Men have two legs just like women, but they walk differently—and usually in different directions: toward bars or football stadiums, for instance. Depending on the cultural stylization, the differences may be stressed or played down; in any case they are not immutable.

Certainly we must respect the rights of those individuals who deviate from the prevailing norms, since every man deviates to some degree from the norm in some trait or other. When it comes to judging people who cannot or do not wish to conform, we should be more protective of the people than the norms. Yet we should not overlook the fact that there is a grain of truth in the norms and in the phrases and clichés that embody them, such as "Face it like a man" or "Every man for himself." Society's overstressing of the norms does not justify the conclusion that the modes of social behavior regarded as typically masculine are purely arbitrary and did not derive from tendencies and characteristics common to all men. Like every other role, the masculine role is certainly just "a sort of mask, a functional construct for behavior toward other people,"[2] but it is no arbitrary concoction; a role can be played successfully only if it "suits" one. Cultural stylization condenses already existing tendencies into authoritative guiding images; it does not freely invent them without regard to reality.

A description of the primordial, fundamental male situation could be summed up in the following five points:

1. Because of the phallic nature of his sex, man has a stronger urge than woman toward expansion in space. His physical constitution codetermines his consciousness. His tendency to orient himself in space, to stake out and defend, and possibly to expand, his own territory stems not from cultural stylization alone but from an innate urge. The territory does not necessarily have to be an area localized in space; it may be completely divorced from spatial reality. It may also be a particular field of work or achievement, manual or intellectual.

2. Because of this attitude, man is the more active social being. To capture and defend his territory he is forced to make alliances and pacts, for no one can win out over everybody else all the time. Since he is the one who has to fight, he is also the one who seeks expedients to make fighting unnecessary. Every territorial fight is bound to take place within existing territories, so that to acquire a territory of his own or a share in a territory, he must first subordinate himself to the existing pecking orders and find his place in them. By staking his claim to a place, he acquires an acknowledged right to expand it.

14

3. This is the origin of man's striving for superior status. The struggle for status is an abstract form of the struggle for territories within a closed social framework. A rise in status nearly always means an automatic expansion of one's territory.

4. Linked with this status struggle are man's order-seeking tendencies: his desire to make laws, to correlate facts in abstract concepts and thus make them manageable.

5. A further consequence is man's need to communicate intellectually with "the whole," with the general public, with the past and the future, to find binding metaphysical orders to sanction and guarantee his laws and covenants, that is to say, his posited norms of moral behavior.

It is not that woman lacks such needs, but that she is both physically less adapted to fighting for territory and status, and psychologically less extroverted. She prefers the center to the frontiers, the conservation and administration of what has already been secured, to the struggle for expansion. It would seem no coincidence that the greatest woman ruler in Western history, the first Queen Elizabeth of England, spent almost all her great abilities in conserving, building, warding off foreign threats, rather than in adventures of expansion. The Drake expeditions were minor aggressions indeed compared with the outward-moving impulses of a Caesar, a Hannibal, a Napoleon or Alexander. Conservation was also the policy, and presumably the temperament, of such great female rulers as Catherine of Russia and Cleopatra. And so, without denying woman's capacity for leadership or opposing her involvement in social, economic, scientific, and other matters formerly closed to her, it appears certain that women, with rare exceptions, tend to act and react differently from men in all such activities. A social reality shaped more by women would certainly look different from what we have, and might indeed look better.

It is a fact, however, that the masculine principle has been dominant in the social and political organization, the scientific and technological development of the great civilizations, even when for dynastic reasons women came to rule. This applies even more categorically to the open global world of our time, the great international structures moving toward world government, a single great world state. Here, a patriarchal impulse is at work.

Yet despite the stirrings of an incipient patriarchal world authority, the traditional male role within society is beginning to lose its validity, in that the conditions of modern industrial society call for a different type of "common man" from that of past history. The traditional male roles no longer fit the realities of masculine life. The great majority of men were, and still are, educated according to codes which are almost impossible to put into practice in our society. The man who still feels bound by them will inevitably find himself in serious conflict situations in everyday life. For this man there are not enough masculine challenges. I do not mean that our world is entirely lacking in man's work or that our society is "effeminate." Nor am I saying that it is no longer possible for our world to produce great men. Indeed, the opposite is true: the world climate cries out for the development of great men; it creates positions of extraordinary, unprecedented power and authority for a few men, yet deprives the vast majority of freedom of decision and action. To put it briefly: Conditions in our world are such that an ever-diminishing number of men can make all the vital decisions for an ever-increasing number of people.

Consider in this connection the order of magnitude of modern mass armies and the technological resources of the dictators who control them. Consider the gigantic power blocs, the great nations and their global range of action. Consider modern political parties and the party bureaucracies whose uncontested power is everywhere invested in a handful of men. The same is true of economic life, with its territorial alliances and pressures from ever-greater unification of economic units. The handful of men at the controls are not necessarily great personalities, yet they are great by virtue of their worldwide power and authority to make decisions. I think it is more than questionable whether individual personalities exist who can exercise this power wisely. Perhaps it is much more difficult than ever before to be a great man; it is certainly becoming more difficult to be a completely ordinary one.

Let us take another look at the male image that we still vaguely think of as the universal criterion. Above all it demands initiative, vigorous, independent action, and the ability to make decisions. Formerly these qualities were required to meet genuine existential needs, primarily in connection

with the establishment and defense of one's own "life territory." Today the little man is relieved of much—perhaps
most—of this by the Big Brothers who have their hands on
the switches and controls of society. His decisions are diverted to secondary areas: to his inward life, to the zone of
play. Only in such a situation could the concept of the playboy become a kind of surrogate image for many young men.
That this image should exist at all among young people shows
how thoroughly the elemental tendency toward self-fulfillment has been shunted into secondary areas of life. Thus the
male becomes an amateur chef or a do-it-yourself interior
decorator; he begins to build things and fix up his house; he
takes sports more seriously than his work; or he turns love
into a game. In what really concerns his existence, in the
shaping of his economic and social environment, he is limited
to voting in an election once every few years. With very
few exceptions the casting of his political vote is all that remains of the exciting freedom of decision, the genuine and
dangerous risking of his whole existence, which traditionally
typified masculine life. And even this survives only for those
who live in liberal, democratic countries. In the so-called
people's democracies, voting itself is a farce.

There is an unbridgeable discrepancy between ideal
and reality, between masculine images and the scope that
real life offers for the development of masculine life. Of
course, the images never coincided completely with actual
modes of life, but they did describe a course for general
conduct, even though the ideals themselves were unattain-

able. Today, however, they point in the wrong direction: back into the past. They offer no usable rules of behavior for contemporary life. Our world does not want the rebellious man who thinks and acts for himself at any risk. Even though it may officially proclaim the opposite for the sake of public relations, the workaday world actually wants the adjustable, adaptable man who can take orders and carry them out. The political world wants the man who swims with the stream, the conscientious voter who is satisfied with the self-commentary of his rulers and offers a minimum of criticism. Calls for political participation always tacitly assume that the potential participant will fit into the existing ideological and organizational setup as smoothly as possible, without obtruding new ideas. The world of commerce wants uncritical buyers and users of its products. Freedom of decision is deflected into the world of play, sports, and tourism, the world of playful eroticism, and to an ever-greater extent, the world of so-called cultural life.

Yet in these fields too, genuine individual participation ranks below mass participation. Although the field of sports still offers the best opportunities for projecting the old male images into real life through such activities as ski jumping, mountain climbing, gliding, parachuting, and scuba fishing, this field also is being increasingly eroded by precautions against the unexpected, by rigorous institutionalization and commercialization. For many men play is becoming more and more of an alternate activity to the battle for territory and status, a battle which is barred from everyday life because there is no scope for it. Yet even in sports, keenness of competition and the increasing measurability of performance are forcing a large proportion of the participants into a passive spectator role, a process to which the perfecting of mass communications media has also contributed. Hence the overwhelming majority of men today give themselves, in their frustration, to passive absorption of the mass media.

A case in point is the extraordinary success of certain types of entertainment, such as the Western and the secret-agent film. Their popularity dramatizes the discrepancy between the historical male role and the average spectator's poor chances of fulfilling it in reality. An article in *The New York Times*[3] on a newly risen star of the Western type, Clint Eastwood, explains that his predominantly male audience admires him as much for his brutality and ruthlessness as for his hippie-like nonconformity. As one admirer said: "He is a real one, all right. The real ones were screwy-looking, stinky types." The author of the article, Aljean Harmetz, goes on to say that "uncountable 40-year-old restaurant owners, barbers, and real estate salesmen have 'never missed a single one' of Eastwood's films." The pithiest reason for this may be found in his wife's comment: "Clint gives the feeling of a man who controls his own destiny."

At the core of such amusements there is obviously a strong element of vicarious gratification. It is an oversimplification to see the average man as a nest of Chinese wooden dolls in which, hidden inside a somewhat overweight white-collar worker in a gray suit, we find one romantic figure after another, until at the very heart of Walter Mitty we come upon James Bond. In reality it is far more complicated; our guiding images permeate reality in a way that cannot be expressed by a metaphor of nesting dolls. The discrepancy between the actual and the ideal person tends to be not a single great gap but a tangle of psychological disjunctions, overlaps, confusions.

In any case, the average man of our time has grave difficulty in reconciling his natural tendencies and his guiding principles with his actual life—far more so than earlier generations. Like the industrial revolution which fostered it, the crisis has accelerated in recent decades. Among a thousand men I have known over the years and in whose lives I have taken an interest, there are remarkably few who have not more than once found themselves in critical conflicts because of the discrepancy between their expectations with regard to the role they accepted for themselves, and the actual circumstances and necessities of their lives. By comparison, women lead lives relatively free from inner conflict. Their problems tend to be with their husbands rather than with their own role in society. Statistics on accidental deaths, executions, suicides, and mental breakdowns list over ten times more men than women. Political and business decisions tend to produce greater conflict, greater nervous strain, with men. Women are usually in a position to give moral support to the men; their involvement being secondary, they can act to mediate and mitigate the conflict. The discrepancy between the role they have to play and the realities of their lives is not so great; sometimes it is so insignificant that they are not even conscious of it.

Man's life appears to be on the way to becoming a sequence of minor and major crises—if not a chronic unbroken crisis—because he has lost the security and protection he used to derive from the old male role. Certainly the female role has changed along with the male role, but in her case the change tends to broaden her existence as a person. The old male role, by contrast, is diminished; indeed it seems to have become completely obsolete, with nothing new to take its place and furnish a guiding code of the same reliability and self-certainty. We have no serviceable, universally recognized image for the passive man. We have no image for the man in retreat, not from the world but from himself in the world. We have no image for the man who adjusts, who submits to circumstances without protest; for the man who is expected to display the one characteristic most contrary to his nature: submission.

The abrogation of the male role is making itself felt in three distinct areas: the erotic sphere, the sphere of male activism and aggressiveness, and finally, the sphere of male authority. Today a man can no longer adhere to the old codes in any of these areas and hope to escape nearly insurmountable conflicts. If he persists in abiding by traditional codes the crisis becomes permanent.

To eliminate these conflicts, should the traditional male role and the patterns of behavior associated with it be discarded and revised to fit existing conditions? Or is it possible to retain the role and change the conditions? To what extent would the roles or the conditions, or both, have to be changed to eliminate the great discrepancies between them? If role behavior is based entirely on cultural stylization, it ought to be possible to recast the male role despite the resistance of traditional mores. The problem would then be one of education and re-education. But if role behavior is instinctual, educational measures could only create a superficial façade and a false consciousness, behind which the old rivalries and territorial struggles would rage in new ways and with quite unpredictable consequences. They could manifest themselves in anything from those furtive but deadly long-term struggles for power within the corporate bureaucracies to the outright catastrophic global war.

A development often predicted for American society, the evolution of "she-men" and "he-women," seems to me neither possible nor practicable.[4] The male world of today, especially some segments of the younger generation, may indeed make an effeminate impression in many ways, but this is deceptive. The "emasculation of our era" is far from total. Perhaps the external signs of effeminacy are a result of intimidation; perhaps they are symptoms of a rising generation's struggle toward a new stylization of roles. Perhaps, though, they are nothing but camouflage for a fight for new freedoms within society—a new form of territorial struggle of an essentially masculine kind. We still know too little about this. Nor would it be true to say that the male world is entirely at the mercy of circumstances. The future is still open.

FIRST SYMPTOM: IMPOTENT ANGER

There may never have been so many men suffering from impotent anger as there are in our time—"anger faint with impotence" is the way Günter Grass puts it. This anger is inarticulate because it does not even know what it wants. Rarely does it reach the point of action, and when it does, the action seems to be other than intended. A rebellion "without a cause" directs itself at random targets, comes to light in mysterious acts of violence, outbursts of blind rage, incoherent criticism, aimless resentment, dreary grumbling, or else in apathetic, helpless, sulky resignation. It takes the forms of car vandalism, office hysteria, marital crises, juvenile delinquency even in well-to-do families, stock market neuroses, student riots, dropping out of school, political and military terrorism—often in response to seemingly arbitrary, accidental, irrelevant provocations. These abrupt precipitates of pent-up aggression, discharged in the wrong place, at the wrong time, at the wrong target, look like grave symptoms of a confusion concealing something other than what they seem to be expressing.

The nature and the causes of anger can most easily be observed in small children. A child will express anger when it fails to get something it wants. Even an infant, denied the warmth and physical closeness of its mother, nourishment,

or the freedom to kick and toss, is capable of violent outbursts of rage. Anger is one of the first and strongest emotions, expressing protest against interference with will and
activity. The only way to prevent anger would be to destroy
the will, especially the will to act. It would be equivalent to
death. Hence it is the task of education not simply to suppress a child's rage, but to show him how to direct his
natural activism into its proper channels, lest unchanneled
energy lead to repressions, blocks, explosions. Conversely,
the causes of seemingly senseless anger and generalized, unfocused resentment must be sought and found, in aid of the
vitality blindly seeking its proper channel.

The foreman who suddenly destroys the punch cards
for the automatic regulation of a steel-rolling machine, the
bank manager tampering with records in order to make them
unusable by a new data processing department, can both
still be understood: these men are fighting the automation
threatening their careers, even though their attack is irrational. There is an obvious connection between the objects
upon which they have chosen to vent their helpless rage and
the processes beyond their reach which they would like to
destroy. But most of the familiar acts of destruction—daily
aspects of the city scene, too numerous to be reported or
even to arouse local comment—no longer reveal any kind of
logic. Demolished park benches, young trees broken or torn
up, trampled flowerbeds on college campuses, broken street
lights and windows, torn and defaced posters, damaged objects of all kinds, bear silent testimony to the pervasiveness
of anger. Among its components, especially in juveniles, is

frustrated activism, love of hunting, longing for adventure, the need to test oneself by taking risks. A surprising proportion of the perpetrators come from decent families, live orderly lives, are regularly employed, and have never before been in trouble with the law. Their actions are merely a more obvious and intense manifestation of widespread patterns of violent behavior evidenced in wanton rowdiness, door slamming, elbowing in buses and subways, abuses on the highways—all outlets in varying degrees of unavowable aggression.

The people who do these things have no understanding of what is driving them. So-called stock market neuroses are usually precipitated by abstract provocations such as rumors, newspaper stories, radio broadcasts, or gossip; not by actual economic emergencies. When a man "flies off the handle" just because he cannot buy his wife a color television set, even though they are well fixed for clothes, food, housing, and comforts such as central heating, he is not acting under the duress of a real emergency; nor does he know what is really troubling him. The same applies to a certain excessive officiousness of petty bureaucrats, what might be called "office neuroses." Without doing anything openly censurable, these bureaucrats tend to harass the person approaching them in their official capacity, keeping him waiting or giving him false or inadequate information, often in a rude manner. By this they seem to be trying to show their power and authority; in reality they are merely revealing their impotence within their organizational setup. They are taking out on their victims their own frustrated activism, driven by subliminal anger which prompts misdirected substitute actions. We are so used to this that we have come to accept it as natural. We tend to be surprised when an official is friendly and helpful, when he gives correct and clear answers even to badly phrased questions. But when he behaves "normally" we leave in a bad temper, repressing our resentment more or less consciously but unconsciously abreacting it somewhere else, or storing it up until at some trivial provocation we explode in a way incomprehensible even to ourselves. And this explosion usually—in fact, nearly always—involves innocent people: subordinates, our own wives and children, individuals who happen to cross our path.

The impotent anger smoldering in our society has long been reflected in angry literature which hits out blindly and violently in all directions, providing an outlet, in a sort of psychological striptease, in stories of monomaniacal suffering, in novels, songs, poems of protest, satiric cabarets, and the theater of the absurd. This literature adds fuel to the smoldering fire, but much of the anger remains aware of its impotence. Literary anger, whether Eastern or Western, is remarkably similar. On a lecture tour in Moscow the American Allen Ginsberg hurls poetic defiance at his own society, while the Russian Andrei Voznesensky does the same in New York.* Their attacks apply to both worlds alike.

* Allen Ginsberg's poem *Howl* (San Francisco: City Lights Books; 1956) was banned for a time; a few weeks after the ban was lifted, it sold five thousand copies. Speaking of the hipsters, the predecessors of the hippies, Ginsberg says:

This literature of impotent wrath first attracted attention in England during the 1950's with such "angry young men" as John Osborne (*Look Back in Anger*) and Colin Wilson (*The Outsider*). In the first quarter of the twentieth century, the anger voiced in literature (as in the Expressionist movement, for example) was predominantly leftist; it sought to change the present for a better future. In the second quarter of the century, a rightist anger came to the fore. Ranging from conservative to reactionary, fostered by the mood of Spengler's *Decline of the West*, it turned away with contempt from the Left's visions of a better future, to praise the lost values of the better past. The anger of the 1950's erupted with a new indignation, regarding the past with loathing, the present with disgust, the future with horror. It was the voice of a generation filled with rage and self-pity because of its impotence.* During this period

---

I saw the best minds of my generation destroyed by madness, starving hysterical naked,

dragging themselves through the negro streets at dawn looking for an angry fix,

angelheaded hipsters burning for the ancient heavenly connection to the starry dynamo in the machinery of night, . . .

who were expelled from the academies for crazy and publishing obscene odes on the windows of the skull,

who cowered in unshaven rooms in underwear, burning their money in waste-baskets and listening to the Terror through the wall . . .

Voznesensky's *Antiworlds* made a great stir in Moscow. The poems were dramatized and aroused so much enthusiasm, especially among Russian youth, that the authorities intervened and Voznesensky's second American tour was canceled.

* Jimmy Porter in John Osborne's *Look Back in Anger* (London: Faber & Faber; 1957) says: "If you've no world of your own, it's rather pleasant to regret the passing of someone else's" (p. 17). And again: "Why don't

28

hordes of literary furies vied in their wholesale attacks upon the establishment and all its works. They saw all governments, past, present, and future, as gangs of criminals. They violently assailed the narrow philistinism of the new working class ("I'm all right, Jack") while at the same time castigating the snobbery and pretentiousness of the rich. They damned the hydrogen bomb and pacifism in the same breath. To them everything conservative was suspect, but everything progressive was absurd. They reviled all religions, yet bemoaned the loss of faith and despised atheism. They rejected democracy but recoiled from totalitarianism. They condemned the intolerance of others but were not noticeably tolerant themselves. And they were only the beginning of a wave of total literary anger which has not yet spent itself.

In the second school of angry literature, that of the American "beat generation," the close connection with actual ways of living is even more evident. Beat literature emerged as an expression of a way of life, a convex mirror presenting a concentrated reflection, and at the same time provided life with new guiding images. When this movement began, there were several thousand beatniks in the United States who had rejected the conventional life of the average American citizen. The beat writers managed to express what these social outsiders felt; they popularized

---

we have a little game? Let's pretend that we're human beings, and that we're actually alive. Just for a while. What do you say? Let's pretend we're human" (p. 15).

the movement's ideas so that it gained many supporters. They initiated the "new youth" life style of today's hippies.*

While this literature reveals extreme self-alienation and an almost total turning away from the world, the impotently angry writers have been vindicated by the success they have achieved in society. Most of them have been attended to, and many have become famous. Their plays are performed, their poems published and eagerly discussed, their novels are widely read and from time to time make the best-seller lists. The literature of anger has succeeded in creating an awareness of the crisis situation at the same time that it serves as a safety valve through which blind resentment can be aired and dissipated.

In fact, the process has reached the point of estheticizing anger, making it powerless and weakening its cathartic effect. A literary avant-garde which cultivates impotent anger must have a masochistic streak in its smugness. The tone is set to an ever-greater degree by male bluestockings. Anger is feminized, deodorized, and made socially acceptable. Impotent anger retreats to a voluble silence, enthusiastically applauded by the critics and by the public it sets out to "annihilate." Many works of angry literature have a strong touch of the cabaret—though often without its enter-

---

* If Allen Ginsberg was the poet of the beat movement, Jack Kerouac was its novelist. In *On the Road* (New York: Viking Press; 1957) the following dialogue occurs between Dean, the beat hero who steals cars out of passion, and the narrator, Sal:
"Whee, Sal, we gotta go and never stop going till we get there."
"Where we going, man?"
"I don't know but we gotta go" (p. 238).

tainment value. And the clowning that goes on in the visual arts is often an exact counterpart of the political warfare that certain activists carry on through journalistic "put-ons." Today's anarchists throw confetti and flowers, not bombs; their literary representatives frequently put their listeners to sleep instead of arousing them. The best of them transcend their impotent rage and enshrine it in the realm of metaphysics.* They retreat to the primal phase of all art: magic incantation. But even in this form, the literary expression of smoldering anger helps to make people aware of the crisis situation and functions as a safety valve. The frustrated are better off because they can identify with what angry literature is saying. By sharing in it they discharge their own unavowed and unrecognized impotent rage.

In day-to-day life as well as in literature, pent-up emotion stemming from constant frustration is usually discharged in words. We are so accustomed to this in ourselves and others that we take it as a matter of course. "So-and-so's in a crabby mood today," we say, or "This is one of his bad days," or "He got out of bed on the wrong side this morning." In such phrases we are objectivizing an indefinable state, applying to it the pseudo-definition "mood," which is then accepted as an act of fate. Often we get some help in dealing with our moodiness from the people around us: members of our family, friends, colleagues, or co-workers

---

* Cf. St.-John Perse's great poem *Exile* (New York: Bollingen Series XV; 1949). In an obvious allusion to the wrath of God as the Bible speaks of it (for instance, in Revelations), St.-John Perse says: *"Je vous dirai tout bas le nom des sources où, demain, nous baignerons un pur courroux"* (p. 29).

grin and bear it. It has almost become a game; there are special rituals for overcoming so-called bad moods which we
are usually not even conscious of because they are so commonplace. With good turns, little courtesies, kindnesses of
one sort or another, we help each other over the rocks of our
"moods." ("I want you to be especially nice to Daddy tonight," a mother will tell her children when her husband
comes home from work after a bad day.) Or we help by
taking people's minds off their worries, distracting them.
("How about a movie tonight? There's a good one playing.") We may use humor to try to get them to laugh
themselves out of it.

A common gambit is to adopt the other person's mood,
add one's own latent resentments to his acute ones, and start
a joint gripe session about "the way things are." Banal purga-
tive rituals of this kind often grow into orgies of abuse
which have an obvious affinity with angry literature. They
may occur when a few workers get together in a factory or
an office, but they develop most frequently in drinking
places. The charge of violent emotion stemming from difficulties which, immediate as they are, seem alien because their
causes are not recognizable, is reversed, as it were, from
negative to positive. Released aggressions are diverted to
visible, concrete circumstances with which one can come
to grips—at least verbally. The gripers can then revile
bureaucracy in general: the whole race of bureaucrats and
managers. Or their abuse may concentrate on democracy:
they may condemn the people's representatives in the legislature for everything that is wrong. The process may also be

more specific: today the Americans may serve as scapegoats, tomorrow the Russians, the blacks, the Reds, the middlemen, the proletariat, the hippies, or the intellectuals. Modern artists are a favorite target.

Thus individuals or groups are singled out as scapegoats for all the evils men suffer, or think they suffer, in the world. Minorities, outsiders, nonconformists of all kinds become the target of a general malevolence. The manager's death from a heart attack, the politician's car wreck, a movie star's suicide, become sources of barely veiled satisfaction for the unsuccessful, whose very insignificance, dependency, and helplessness can thus be felt as assets. Certain clichés of general resentment, such as *"They* do as they please with *us,"* "Nobody asks *us,"* *"We* have no say in this," provide a kind of informal ritual of discharge, a vent for relieving pent-up hostility. In such verbal release, the actual causes of the "bad mood" can be momentarily forgotten; frustration is overcome, anger dissipated in generalities.

Our cultural life offers many officially authorized events that serve as diversionary outlets. We seldom realize what an important function they have in this respect, because we associate them with sports, pleasure, and entertainment. But the emotions expressed by crowds in football stadiums, at boxing matches, or at rock 'n roll concerts are not aroused purely by the play instinct; they are not wholly a response to what is actually going on. These events are in a great degree outlets for already existing tensions. The pent-up emotion the spectators bring with them is linked only functionally with the events, which in reality serve to give these blocked emotions an approved avenue of escape.

This becomes clear when we compare the essentially trivial stimuli with their tremendous effects. The movements of a pigskin ball, the contest of two wrestlers, the music played by a rhythm band cannot in themselves cause thousands of people to become so excited that they demolish seats and bleachers or beat up individual players, referees, and fellow spectators. Explaining the necessity for the huge detachments of police on duty at sports events, a top football official once said: "You never know when and where the anger of the common people is going to break out!" Such matches are actually hostility rituals, abstracted from real social warfare, that permit the discharge of violent emotions for which normal life provides insufficient scope. Most people, of course, are aware of the "play" quality of these mass events: they do not seriously mean the insults they hurl at the players, or even their own acts of physical violence. When such affairs end in a rampage, nobody is more surprised than the participants—they "don't know what got into them."

This smoldering anger does not always find such direct outlets. It often remains unfocused, turns into grumbling resignation, sublimates itself in petty meanness in the daily routine, or loses itself completely in generalities. It spills out in political attitudes or cultural behavior patterns; in class ideologies, aversions to specific nationalities and races; in romantic postures such as the rejection of progressive technology or the utopian rejection of all tradition. However purposeful such one-sided attitudes may seem, they all too

34

often lack any foundation; the principles on which they claim to be founded turn out to be a subterfuge. This applies equally to terrorists of the Right and those of the extreme Left; in both cases subliminal aggression and an insufficiently analyzed "uneasiness" are short-circuited and directed toward substitute ends. Radical reactionary groups believe that their goals are firm and that they understand the reasons for their actions. So do the radical "progressive" groups, whose antifascist motivation leads them to spend themselves fighting the "reactionaries" instead of devoting themselves to constructive tasks. But everywhere the real causes are masked; the outburst of aggressiveness is directed at substitute, more or less random targets selected for the purpose of discharging pent-up anger and escaping from the extraordinary uncertainty of purpose that is universal in today's social climate. Behind the mask, however, lie obscure psychic and social tensions quite different from the ones expressed.

SECOND SYMPTON: THE ABSURDIST REVOLT

Since the mid-1950's there has been a spate of sensational news stories about striking new modes of behavior among groups of young people. These groups are known by many different names: frivolous *vitelloni* and indolent *lazzaroni* in Italy; dandified Teddy Boys, elegant mods, and wild rockers in England; hippies in the United States; violent *rag-*

gares and blatantly made-up *maskots* in Sweden; aggressive *provos* in Holland; pleasure-seeking *hooligans* in the Eastern European countries; and unwashed *Gammler* and *Halbstarke* in Germany. In most industrialized areas of Europe, even in the Communist hemisphere, new ways of life are emerging in which, local and national differences notwithstanding, young people see themselves as attempting to escape from or break through the conventional forms of industrial life. Today's teenagers and young adults have been called rebellious, loud, hedonistic and dissipated, maladjusted, uninhibited, and extreme, but no satisfactory interpretation of their behavior has been proposed. Does a new generation really arise every few years? Or are all these groups linked by some common factor? Is there, as has been suggested, such a thing as a new life style for youth?

The trend toward new modes of life is most conspicuous in the United States, where hundreds of thousands of hippies have succeeded the beatniks of the 1950's, those nonconformists who refused to pursue the almighty dollar or wear a clean shirt every day, who hung their gray-flannel suits in the closet, bought themselves blue jeans, shabby sweaters, and sandals in thrift shops, and dropped out of society. In the midst of ever-increasing affluence the beatniks lived a life opposed to competition for the dollar and preached asceticism so far as consumer goods were concerned. Renouncing personal and social ambitions, they lived as hoboes, beggars, drifters, thereby dramatizing their rejection of the technotronic society's conventional life patterns.

Where the costumes of American nonconformists tend, not toward the minimal or ascetic, but toward decoration and ornaments, they nevertheless reflect some form of opting-out of the existing society. Young people may rifle their parents' attic for "granny clothes" or Edwardian finery, may go in for old-fashioned hand-knit or crocheted styles, or may try for a gypsy, tribal Indian, or African effect. Throughout the world there is by now a wide spectrum of such anti-establishment, anti-status-quo costumery that may have nothing in common except a shared rebelliousness. American beats and hippies led the way, but they were soon emulated by the young everywhere, including Moscow and the Third World.

The designation "beatnik" suggests a programmatic identification with the "beaten-down" element of society. It is well to remember, however, that Jack Kerouac explained "beat" as derived from the same Latin root that gave us "beatific" and "beatitude," and thus as containing in one syllable the New Testament's message "Blessed are the poor" and the implied program of the beats to inherit the earth in their own negative way. This program, apparently without system but not without method, includes dropping out of the rat race, doing nothing, embracing poverty. It is a program that has been followed by individuals throughout history, but as a movement has usually involved religious, otherworldly ends. For the beats and flower children, no transcendental ends beyond this world and this life are in view. Nevertheless, the rejection of material goods and the tuning in to the universe, usually by means of special stimulants but also with the help of music, incantation, and ritual strongly under Eastern influence, aims at nothing less than experiencing eternity, by way of an infinite extension of the sense of life, while still inside one's human skin.

As regards the political and social implications of such a life style, it would have to be a socialism as close as possible to anarchy, to be achieved without a party organization, without a bureaucracy, without leaders or even an explicit fixed program. Since these rebels are straining to escape from history altogether, they can oppose everything at once: democracy, fascism, monarchy, and revolution itself. Their utopia is a loose, uninstitutionalized collectivism totally permissive toward the individual. Meanwhile they wage war upon the prevailing worship of consumer goods by practicing asceticism, and upon a hypertrophied society by practicing anarchism.

It is not likely that the style, the language, the outlook of the beats and the flower children would have rubbed off as it did—even on those consciously out of sympathy with them—if it did not represent a deeper, broader stratum, a general tendency among the "squares." And the tremendous publicity these young rebels and absurdists have achieved through the popular media suggests that they are far from being regarded as mere eccentrics, or their movement as a negligible phenomenon. Possibly many of the so-called squares who shave every day and get to work on time, wearing a clean shirt and a tie, are disenchanted with the ideas and aims of the establishment, and ready to see absurdity where the young rebels see it. Perhaps the majority that feels constrained to go along with the power structure are expressing their alienation, their failure to find meaning in it apart from its naked survival value, by keeping their eyes and ears on the rebels through the media.

Despite all the apparent inconsistencies in the ideology and conduct of the rebels, a number of their basic postulates can be identified. One is connected with personal appearance: the emphasis on looking free. This, incidentally, strikes a blow against Madison Avenue and its commercial insistence on a personal hygiene dependent upon such touted products as soap, razors, and cosmetics. An inconsistency might be seen in the loving attention lavished on their long hair by some men who appear negligent about their clothing and their cleanliness. But the paradox is only superficial: the movement is toward the natural, such as letting one's hair grow, against the artificial conformity of such styles as the crew cut. And long hair on a man has traditionally been a sign of freedom: in antiquity only slaves had to be uniformly shorn; in the middle ages only serfs; and today only the convict, the soldier, and the industrial worker whose beard and long hair might be a hazard to him among machinery and flying sparks.

Along with the conformist middle-class look, the rebel rejects the standard bourgeois living arrangements. Hippies live communally, sharing what little they possess; avoiding the fixities of permanent homes, the baggage of superfluous possessions; content if they have a mattress to sleep on, a hotplate for cooking. They do not make a fetish of consistency: while they dismiss such a product of technology as the refrigerator because it is a symbolic ritual object of the despised bourgeois marriage, they do not reject a record player with its complement of rock records.

Thirdly, and this is particularly noteworthy, they postulate their right to take love as a game. Beat philosophy had already derived this doctrine from progressive sex psychology, opposing not only the bourgeois marriage but all fixed forms of sexual life. If human instincts are not the unchanging entities they were once thought to be, and sexual characteristics, male and female, exhibit a great range of variation, then the norm is only a statistical, not a moral, concept, and every deviation from it is equally valid and permissible. In the interests of individual freedom, of creative variety, departures from the norm are rather to be encouraged than otherwise. Hence group love, flexible pairing arrangements, open promiscuity are legitimate on the hippie scene. While stable domestic arrangements are not uncommon or discouraged in the drop-out generation, there need be no connection between sexual gratification and procreation, between indulgence and responsibility. Hippies are not disturbed that the new sexual freedom, which incidentally militates against the growth of deep and lasting emotional relationships, depends largely on scientific methods of birth control which could have been achieved only within the highly disciplined technotronic society they claim to reject.

In the hippie world such inconsistencies and depressing realities are commonly bypassed with the aid of drugs and intoxicants meant to transport the user into infinities of freedom and joy, without any need for thought or effort. The temptation to renounce reality altogether may become irresistible, even when the growth of drug addiction does not lead to psychosis and thereby forcibly deprives the user of his last contact with reality. In either case, frustration and impotent anger were the starting point of the absurdist rebellion against reality.

In these young rebels, there is actually a great deal of Samuel Beckett's tragic clowns. They tend to act out in life their own theater of the absurd. But "absurd" theater is not absurd: it exposes and questions the absurdity of human existence. In Beckett's *Waiting for Godot*, which long antedates the American hippie movement, two unwashed vagabonds are endlessly waiting for something to happen. They do not know what they are waiting for or what they want, but they want it desperately and immediately. This is precisely the psychological situation of the absurdist rebels, except that it is part of a deliberate choice. Their aim is to turn life into art, art into life. Kinetic art, pop art, the "happening"—all exemplify this aim. The happening in particular seeks to stimulate and heighten experience as a work of art does, while remaining an unpremeditated, free-flowing, aimlessly uncontrolled bit of real life. The hippie be-in, with its costume-party theatricality, is the communal equivalent.

Pop art, kinetic art, happenings, body painting, tribalism, cannot be dismissed as passing fads. The disintegration of our closed ideological superstructures is making room for a new relationship with objects, unconsciously magical in

character. The hippie's object fetishism, his mania for col-
lecting and hanging all sorts of things on his neck and limbs,
all add up to an unconscious experimentation with symbolism. That the objects tend to be trashy looking—things of no
market value such as bits of colored glass, pebbles, shells, old
bottles, rags, tin message buttons—reflects the revolt against
the media-bred consumer psychology that seeks the new
model, the high-priced gadget, only to devour it and turn it
into waste. Instead, these objects are valued for themselves,
for having a past or suggesting one, as do granny spectacles
and granny dresses, or having a story, such as German steel
helmets, Iron Crosses, Hindu emblems. Thus they possess a
being of their own which gives them power to invoke nature,
or history, or antiworlds. Even non-sense, the power of the
irrational, is thus called upon against the superrationalized
power structure; all is fair in this fight of the powerless
against overwhelming odds. The flamboyant theatrical note
in the hippie's dressing "down" can be seen as a flourish of
defiance against his own helplessness. Lacking power, one
tries to prevail by means of charm, or charms; to hypnotize
the enemy by display, gesture, ritual, spectacle; to disarm him
by being demonstratively harmless, as when one hands a
flower to a cop. The objective of one's revolt remains this:
to find or create a living self and keep it from being "auto-
mated" in the sense of being turned into an automaton obedient to the socio-economic machinery.

Movement as such is another striking factor in the
hippie revolt. The emphasis on rhythm, on "a good beat," the
love of dancing in general—and in particular of rock 'n roll

and primitive dance, of a kind of dance that is both communal and "permissive" of individual improvisation—are all part of this urge toward a free play of energy, a free art of energy. Some of the dances suggest the behavioralists' formulation of "going through the motions of flight while remaining rooted to the spot." There is an element of humor in them: such dances demonstrate purposelessness as an antidote to the tyrannical purposiveness of the workaday and career world; they exhibit a playful squandering of energy, an unprecedented amount of which has been released in our time from socio-economic enslavement. A new mobile society is emerging from the old "sedentary" culture and finding its most vigorous expression in the neoprimitive social dancing of our discotheques.

A related development is the emergence of new social ideals, a new kind of group life, "tribal cultures" rising up in the very midst of technotronic civilization. Half in play, these groups seek new cults, new rituals, a new etiquette to emphasize and seal the opposition to the old society. The youth movement's view that society is one great prison and that a society of the future must have more room for play is not to be understood as merely a shunning of responsibility. It stems rather from the lack of free scope for action within the existing society, and from youth's consciousness of far greater physical energies than ever before. But political revolution alone is not enough; there is a utopian longing for a revolt of the total man, for a "return" to an unalienated humanity in harmony with nature, to pretechnological ideals and ways of life. This viewpoint does not take into account that to reject industrial progress is to destroy the actual basis of existence.

The current global youth movement appears to be the most disoriented revolt of all time. In it all extremes meet; progressive utopians and reactionary romantics find common ground, offering to improve society by addressing themselves directly to the quality of human life itself. But without a systematic understanding of what needs to be changed and how, without methodological agreement, they can never achieve effective political action. Feeling impelled and obliged to act, they do so in a blindly improvised manner that tends to blur all traditional distinctions between progress and reaction. They can sympathize with Communism, with the emergent nationalism of the Third World, with the struggles of the American blacks, but cannot be expected to support any practical implementations that must involve machinery, organizations, institutionalization, even guns. One of the cruelest inconsistencies plaguing these opponents of aggression and advocates of total tolerance, including tolerance for such traditional outsiders as homosexuals and criminals, is the unintended aggression and intolerance that results from their stance. For example, their refusal to work and thereby to support any further wars also precludes their taking a share in supporting social security for the aged—a rather inhumane abrogation of responsibility that belies their vociferous proclamations of universal humanity. This illustrates the well-known psychological fact that attitudes and even practices of self-abnegation do not necessarily make men more humane; they too often serve to sanction severe aggression against others. Meanwhile our growing indebtedness to the future is alarming. The demagogic irresponsibility with which most governments squeeze ever-higher tax contributions out of the income-producing segments of society arouses justifiable resistance.

All the rebels unanimously reject the existing form of society as senile. They all object in principle to three generally accepted foundations of society: the moral obligation to work, middle-class marriage, and the bureaucratic and military power of the state. Many of them implement these views by dropping out of the production-consumption cycle, repudiating marriage ties in favor of free love and promiscuity, refusing to serve in the Army, and protesting against war and the use of force in general, such as by the police and the prison system.

The logic of this program depends on the basic belief that all the evil in the world could be eliminated if we renounced the use of force and got rid of whatever might provoke it. The rebel says, in effect: "By not producing, you're not contributing to the rat race for consumer goods. By not owning anything, you destroy the breeding ground of envy. By not monopolizing another person's love, you eliminate a source of potential conflict. You're not open to jealousy. You don't have to drudge to provide for others. You can drop out of the production-consumption cycle. You don't have to fight for anybody." In this way, they think, they can rid the world of explosive issues, and in the process the state and its institutions will automatically lose their justification. If nobody is forced to call upon state institutions for protection, the state can make no demands on its citizens and hence will not commit aggression against the citizens of other states.

The proponents of this ideology fail to see themselves as entirely conditioned by the industrial society they attack, which not only bred them but made their way of life and even their thinking possible. Committed as they are to the old Rousseauist fallacy that man is by nature good and is corrupted only by social conditions, they want to change these conditions radically. They often do so in irrational, self-destructive ways, and threaten to turn the Promethean revolt—defined by Camus as a revolt against the absurd and therefore a revolt to give meaning to the absurd—into a revolt in favor of meaninglessness. But illogic may also be used as a defense against subjugation and oppression. We can postulate, along with Camus, that "every revolt invokes a value." We can then see the absurdist revolt as a new ferment in the industrial world, both Eastern and Western, produced by a movement which is more elemental, more violent, perhaps indeed considerably less humane than its proponents realize. The "invoked value" of the absurdist revolt of youth lies in the fact that it is a manifestation, occurring within contemporary conditions but stemming from elemental modes of human behavior, of a male impulse toward freedom. It proves that even in an almost totally institutionalized, managed, overorganized society, man feels a compulsive need to fight for free domains offering new possibilities for initiative, where there will be scope for his spontaneity.

2

THE CRISIS OF EROS

Of the three decisive areas of life in which the traditional male role has noticeably changed or even become obsolete, the erotic sphere is only one. Acute as the disturbances in this sphere may be, their causes lie elsewhere; nor is it a question of a decline in sexual potency as such. On the contrary, the male today may well surpass previous generations in health and physical strength, owing to improved nutrition, hygiene, and medical care, as well as the proliferation of sports. The disturbance is clearly psychological in origin, and affects the will, consciously or not. The male crisis does not originate in the sexual sphere; it erupts there, being caused by general social conditions governing relations between the sexes and by disturbances in areas other than that of sex.

Paradoxically, perhaps the most conspicuous and truly alarming sign of a disturbed Eros is the ever-broadening wave of overt sexuality sweeping across industrial society. A flood of sexy song hits and posters, sex movies, sex magazines and books pervades our public life. Never in any era has the public been so inundated with sex signals and stimuli. It is futile to argue that erotic art has always existed in the most diverse eras and cultural milieus, for insofar as it is genuine art (even though it may cross the borderline of what we call pornography), erotic art has always reflected a general cultural or personal encounter with facts of erotic life. In contrast to today's sex boom and its worldwide flaunting of bosom and skin fetishism, even the openly displayed genital eroticism of Pompeiian frescoes and the reliefs in the temples of Konarak and Khajuraho in southern India obviously belong to an intimate life setting or to ritualistic cults. But erotic art, although it has been reproduced in books, does not lend itself to infinite reproduction as a consumer commodity. Works of art, even though they are bought and sold, are not intrinsically merchandise purely for consumption; they stimulate psychological reactions. The sex wave of today, by contrast, is a kind of clearance sale, offering shabby goods at bargain prices. Its overproduction of erotic stimuli as merchandise produces an inflation of Eros. Even the international use of the word "sex" is revealing, implying some internationally recognized standard of currency.

It is, without doubt, the remarkable expansion of our ever-improving reproduction techniques that is responsible for the industrialization and manipulation of Eros itself. Sexual stimuli can now be reproduced on a scale never before possible. In their extraordinary proliferation they become banal; they are revalued—and in a sense devalued. Modern reproduction techniques also lead to depersonalization, as shown by a glance at our posters, magazines, display windows, and movies. Generalized sex loses the unique quality of personal erotic encounter. To put it metaphorically, Eros today does not await a suitable opportunity to shoot his arrows at individual targets; he showers them blindly on society as a whole, or rather bombards it with a barrage of "sex-bombs" and out-size bosoms, keeping it in a permanent state of sexual excitement and even overexcitement. It says much for the amazing biological indestructibility and vitality of human sexuality that this has not yet led to any noticeable debilitation or deterioration of potency.

There can be little doubt that the sex wave is manipulated by man, not woman. Visually, sex symbolism tends to express itself in terms of the female physique. A characteristic feature of the current wave is the ever-increasing exposure of the parts of the female body that are particularly exciting sexually. The rule has been, until very recently at least, for female rather than male nudity to be on display; there is as yet no "Playgirl" magazine featuring male beauty in the nude. Men pictured naked must be shown engaged in some sport such as boxing, weight lifting, wrestling, diving. While feminine lingerie plays a prominent part in advertising, men's underwear is kept discreetly in the background, in ads not designed for their stimulating effect on women. Nude men in sex films tend to appear in the role of an indispensable accessory, much like the purely supportive male ballet dancer, with the main interest focused on the female body.

It is men who create the pictures, photographs, and

films that make woman and her sexual attributes into a commodity. To do this they obviously need women, and plenty of women are ready to cooperate by becoming models, mannequins, and extras promoting sex. But the directors, cameramen, and producers of sex movies are all men. The woman widely considered the most outstanding in movie-making today, Agnès Varda, has always been very conservative, even when dealing with contemporary sexual problems. In the visual arts no woman has ever used pornography as an artistic medium: there are no obscene drawings by women of men's or boys' bodies, and throughout art history women have produced no parallel to life studies of female models. Although this does not necessarily mean that women are less interested in the male body than vice versa, it does mean that men's interest in the female body is different in kind from women's interest in the male. What attracts the man is the pointing up of visual stimuli that excite him and prompt direct sexual activity—stimuli that arouse his virility. Sexual activity in women, by contrast, is aroused much more by the man's activity. To put it antithetically, the male body is interesting to the woman only in action, whereas the mere sight of nude female beauty in repose may be enough to arouse a man. Indeed, paintings of the female nude would seem to suggest that the naked female body in repose is the greatest challenge man knows.

In general, mobilized femininity persistently calls attention to sexual attractions heightened to the extreme. And no era has ever displayed feminine charms so openly or so universally as ours. Women imitate the behavior of movie stars and models, constantly provoking the male without even meaning to or being aware of it, always "promising" something they can never deliver. This forces man into a kind of voyeur position; he is continually being challenged to look, even though the challenge is not addressed to him personally. Constantly confronted with sex signals as obvious as if they were part of an advertising display, he reacts like the well-drilled recruit who, seeing a general's uniform, automatically salutes, only to find that his courtesy was addressed to a dummy in a military outfitter's show window. The male feels stimulated and personally challenged, when actually he is merely the victim of a state of affairs which the masculine world itself has created. And while the women may believe that they have obligingly accommodated themselves to this in order to gain their own ends, they are really being manipulated too.

It is man who prostitutes the female body by displaying it ever more freely and exhibitionistically. Everywhere we turn we see men in the role of pimps, offering feminine sexual charms as merchandise, either as a straight sexual commodity or as merchandise of some other kind packaged as sex. Thus woman's essential significance as the object of male sexual desire undergoes a change. By accommodating herself to masculine sex instincts, she becomes an object of the male struggle for profit, status, and territory. Incessantly advertised sex symbols, reproduced in such a multiplicity of forms, mobilize sexuality on a prodigious scale, transfer it from the private to the public sphere and allow it no latency. They take sex out of the obscure realm of sleep and dreams and plunge it into a reality which demands unremitting action. Yet this constant mobilization of sex is merely a cover for something else. The fetish of sex is nothing but a camouflaged fetish of a kind of consumer goods.

The last continent to be exploited is neither the deep sea nor outer space, but the realm of sex. Sex is the biggest business of the century, the last remaining colony, profitable and unresisting. Industries, great and small, live on it; many —in fact most—other fields of production serve its cause. With the help of the mass media, countless individuals make enormous profits out of sex: by exploiting the sexual domain as film stars and singers, and sometimes as writers, they become millionaires. They all prostitute themselves or other people, turning sex into a commodity. Yet only the small-time operators, such as registered prostitutes or artists branded as pornographers, are ostracized or, occasionally, kept under police surveillance and prosecuted. Meanwhile sex is booming; the Pope gives his blessing to mini-skirted sexpots, and Hollywood controls its own censors so that the American film industry will not be handicapped in the world market. The whole boom amounts to a monstrous distortion of sex, which, besides being divorced from its traditional, often outdated, cultural stylizations, loses vital elements of its natural constitution. By being made part of the battle-ground of commercial competition, it is seriously alienated from its true nature. For this process leads to a change of consciousness: generalized sex is divorced in the human consciousness from the person-to-person erotic relationship. Even if in practice this divorce remains incomplete because, when all is said and done, personal encounter is still a stronger force in life than any abstraction, the sex wave nevertheless makes it harder to establish and maintain a personal erotic relationship.

We think we are considerably above those early cultures in which, as the ethnologists tell us, woman was merely a barter object for men. (We may note in passing that it was always the men who did the bartering, not the woman.) As general morality evolved, it more or less eliminated the trading and selling of women and frowned on the open abuse of sex as a commodity. The attitude now survives only indirectly in the socially outlawed back alleys of prostitution. Nevertheless, by a great detour our era has succeeded in turning sex back into a commodity, though admittedly in an abstract form in which it is marketed as a stimulus, not a gratification. However far they go, even if they publicize the most intimate zones of the body or the most intimate acts, including even their own acts of coitus (as has already been done in films), the men and women who sell these reproduced stimuli still regard themselves as blameless. They feel they are selling a reproduction, not themselves. But the public's consciousness is nevertheless vitally affected: essentially the actors become guiding images for other people, and by making their own intimate behavior available as a commodity, they suggest to the public that sex is indeed merchandise.

The current sex boom thus represents something very different from what twentieth-century sexual philosophers and reformers had in mind. Instead of liberating man from

53

overstrict conventions which conflict with the findings of modern sexual research, the involvement of Eros in consumer-goods fetishism and in the conspicuous waste of the economic process has produced a new alienation and new pressures.

What forces activate the sex wave? Does the responsibility lie with advertising men and the entertainment industry? Does it also fall on those technicians of applied psychology who have utilized the findings of modern sexology in marketing their wares? In the last analysis, was it the sexologists and sex reformers themselves who started the sex wave, simply as a result of their concentration on this aspect of human life?

Any such answers would be oversimplifications, of course. The sex wave is an outgrowth of the total complex of contemporary industrial life, which includes the reproducibility of goods and services in massive volume. This almost automatically entails the constant expansion of markets and a ceaseless search for new raw materials to be processed and distributed at a profit. Certainly so inexhaustible a "raw material" as sex, capable of being offered in so many forms—real, imaginary, even illusory—in a pre-sold market, could hardly have been long overlooked. By demolishing existing sexual taboos, the sexologists quite incidentally contributed their share to the commercialization of sex. Despite the initial violent opposition to their more iconoclastic tenets, the net result of their "pure research" and disinterested scientific investigations was highly beneficial to the commercial exploitation of sexuality. This was not at all what Sigmund Freud had intended! Yet even before Freud, the Copernicus of the libido, had been recognized and become socially acceptable, his theories had begun to change the market all along the line. It was the market that took over sex, not the other way around. What we call the sexual freedom of contemporary society is at least as much the result of the commercialization of sex as of any process of scientific enlightenment. Indeed, because of the commercialization of sex, the struggle for sexual freedom seems to be leading to new forms of sexual duress, including new constraints which are producing new distortions.

Our sex reformers, still inveighing against the gray sickness of puritanism, against asceticism, repression, and sexual dishonesty, present a comic spectacle in a world where billboards, newspapers, magazines, films, and increasingly even radio and television discard sexual taboos in wholesale lots. The conservative forces for "moral cleanliness" and "protection of youth" against pornographic "filth and trash" are only covering a retreat, not to say a rout. The progressive sexologists, tilting at windmills, believe they are knights crusading against the hypocrisy of society's moral façade. But what we think of as public morality has long been a farce, a kind of mask which at best heightens the attraction of the sexual game. The traditional bridal white, for example, has long since lost its original connotation of virginity. Nowadays people are more inclined to think that it is hard for a virgin to get a husband. Virginity has come to signify, not virtue or purity but, if it is too prolonged at least, a kind of failure.

Because of the commercialization of sex and the incessant bombardment of the public with sexual stimuli, real or symbolic, sex has acquired an exaggerated significance. A consumer mentality toward sex has been created which bears very little relation to the liberation from puritanism the sexologists originally intended. As a result, the role of the theoreticians of sex is changing into that of functionaries and agents for the market, as they themselves become objects of industrial exploitation.

Like another series of phenomena which we shall discuss later, the sex wave is a consequence of man's imprisonment in the "unnatural conditions" created by industrial progress. These conditions are irreversible; even political revolutions cannot get rid of them. Communism has not been able to eliminate the consumer-goods fetishism that stems from industrial conditions, but only to postpone it. Since this fetishism is a psychological consequence of mass production, upon which we depend, we cannot prevent it. If we regard the sex wave as a result of our industrial culture, it is man-made. Total sexual mobilization is, accordingly, part of the masculine manipulation of the world, through which a segment of the male population is maneuvered into a pimping role, even though men find this role irritating and profoundly threatening to their virility.

We can speak, then, of a setting for massive male neurosis. The extensive liberation of sexuality from the biological and social context of life so that it is little more than a lustful end in itself comes far more naturally to the male than the female. While films, television, magazines, popular music, and advertising act to sexualize the current scene, contraceptive know-how perfects the subjective divorce of sex from responsibility both toward the other individual and toward society. Sex is thus "freed" to be a consumer commodity, and while completely open, unrestricted promiscuity is still reserved to an elite of the happy few as it always has been, for the first time in history it can be preached to the multitudes as a highly moral and desirable course to follow. The slogan "Make love, not war" carried in so many parades advertises love making in general as a cure-all for society's gravest ills. As a result, there are people who put up a front of complete sexual freedom in their lives; chastity or personal fidelity has become something to justify and apologize for. Love is a casual social game conducted publicly in a misconceived carnival spirit the year around. What used to be an upper-class prerogative in periods of decadence has been democratized, opened to the general public and is flaunted by the young.

The individual capacity for love is a kind of capital which can be invested, spent, or frittered away. To flirt with the possibilities of love, to explore them and experiment with them, has always been the privilege of youth, even when the limits were more strictly defined than they are today. Now, however, experimentation in love has become an end in itself. The experimental posture is presented as the normal one, while fixation upon a single love object for a protracted period of time is suspect. This is not disproved by the fact that marriages, even young marriages, still take place and that a good many of them last. On the whole, marriages

57

are felt to be far less binding than they were, entered into with far more reservations by both partners. Consciously or not, the possibility of breakup, separation, and divorce shadows the marriage contract and, more often than not, remains in faithful attendance throughout the life of the marriage.

Such an attitude enables one to circumvent the problems that arise in the course of deepening an erotic relationship into an enduring personal bond, and even to avoid deepening it altogether. Thus the desire for personal intimacy inherent in the sexual relationship is fulfilled ever more cursorily. The relationship remains superficial, relying on a quick succession of increasingly cruder, shallower sensations. More and more it tends to be relatively indiscriminate, readily initiated, easily dropped or exchanged for a "newer model."

In this situation sexual behavior acquires, paradoxically, a new look of playfulness while underneath it has a new grimly serious quality. Schelsky in fact declares that sex in our day has lost its playfulness. Like football, our equivalent of the gladiatorial contests of ancient Rome, it has become a commodity to be taken in deadly earnest: "Just as the apparently free consumer, exercising his apparently free choice, has long been driven by the lash of terroristic sales methods to want what he is supposed to want; just as he invests his quasi-freedom in controlled business activity in a planned, prearranged way; so the quest for sexual pleasure has long since become a quasi-compulsory kind of personal and social activity in which the carefree quality of play is totally lost."[1] But this conclusion is justified only to the extent that play is presumed to be carefree, whereas any casual observation of a group of children at play demonstrates that a game must be played seriously to be played at all. A more indisputable characteristic of play, perhaps, is that one is free to drop out, and that a game can be broken off and a new one begun at any time. In this respect much of contemporary sex activity can indeed be regarded as a game.

And yet I see something quite different as the most essential trait of the sexual behavior of our time. Precisely because it offers so much room for "play," it allows impulses and modes of behavior originating elsewhere to be channeled into the sexual sphere, which then has to accommodate them. For one thing, there appears to be a new aggressiveness in sexual behavior today. Not that aggressiveness in sex is an altogether alien element, as the expression "battle of the sexes" testifies. But the natural aggressive component has received reinforcements from other areas in the human and social psyche. Such an invasion of the sexual sphere by something grown in another soil is illustrated by the figure of Don Juan, who was actually a fourteenth-century phenomenon. He did not become famous, however, until the seventeenth and eighteenth centuries, when the image of the playboy became the accepted self-image of an aristocracy that was losing its social function, subsiding into decadence, and transferring its social aggressiveness to the sexual sphere in the symbolic person of the all-conquering Don Juan. Today's male youth performs a similar transfer of male aggressiveness from the socio-economic sphere to the sexual. In *The Red and the Black*, Stendhal's Julien Sorel carries the social struggle of an ambitious middle class with an aristocratic establishment into the bedchamber; he "makes it" by sleeping with Mathilde, the daughter of the marquis who is Julien's employer. In the last quarter of the nineteenth century Strindberg, the "son of a servant," portrayed in *Miss Julie* and *The Dance of Death* the interlinked social struggle of the advancing proletariat, the battle of the sexes, and the complexities of emancipation for the women of an individualistic middle class.

But nowhere in literature, not even in these exceptional cases, does the "battle of the sexes" stem exclusively from the sexual relationship between man and woman. Even though romantic literature (E. T. A. Hoffmann's *Don Juan*, for instance) heightens the sexually aggressive figure of Don Juan to a "sensuality beyond the sensual," it is obvious that the problem is posed in this way for the sake of dramatic effect and that excessive sexual activity and aggressiveness serve to compensate for other impulses. Biologically, aggressiveness between the sexes plays a modest role. In early cultures, the rape and abduction of women tended to be ritualized, institutionalized events rather than an expression of natural, primitive aggressiveness. Today a new importance has come to be attached to aggression in sexual behavior, an increased emphasis which may indicate a displacement of surplus aggression from other spheres. As Karen Horney points out, "A great deal of sexual activity today is more an outlet for psychic tensions than a genuine sexual drive, and is therefore to be regarded more as a sedative than as genuine sexual enjoyment or happiness."[2] The development of the detective story from Conan Doyle to Mickey Spillane sufficiently illustrates the increasing interest in sexual violence. In books, films, even the theater, hostility and aggressive cruelty in the sex act (an element which normally represents genuine playfulness, a ritual pointing up of the final purpose of the act, which is to give and find satisfaction) seems almost to become an end in itself.

We find many examples of this false conception of sex in literature. Hemingway's Harry in *The Snows of Kilimanjaro* refers to sexual intercourse as "the good destruction." Robert Musil, that rational mystic of the sexual life, explores the ecstasies and abysses of sexual encounter and through exemplary situations reveals them in a way almost no other novelist has managed to do. In the concluding notes for his unfinished novel *The Man Without Qualities* Musil gives his hero this despairing thought, now that all his relationships have foundered: "Last resort: sexuality and war. But sex only lasts a night. War probably a month. And so on."[3] Anticipating what is to come, aggression in war and aggression in sex are fully equated. A Swedish student recently made this statement: "In other countries people kill each other. In Sweden we sleep together." What Ernst Junger calls "the glorious madness of the blood" of the fighting man-beast is carried over directly into sex with no apparent need of emotional or moral transition.[4] "Sleeping" together is akin to killing one another; war and sex boil down to the same thing.

An attitude like this turns woman into a shock absorber for man's defiant ferocity, which originally served quite different purposes. Some of the aggression that used to be invested chiefly in the struggle for life (i.e., in social and national conflicts) is transposed into or superimposed on the sexual life as bed "fighting." The meaning of the sexual act shifts from the experience of union toward constantly reiterated disunion. The dominant pattern is one of resistance and conquest, not wooing and yielding. What the continually repeated game of finding and losing stands for within the erotic relationship becomes, in the purely sexual relationship, a sort of all-out wrestling contest which recognizes only stronger and weaker, oppression and rebellion, victory or defeat. The sex act is carried out like a military operation.

This inherent convertibility of the male aggressive impulse, now heightened to the point of viciousness; this shifting of the brutal lust for power and domination from the social realm into the sexual, has been described in extreme crisis situations by the Marquis de Sade, one of the great unmaskers of man's corruptible nature. Ludwig Marcuse testifies to this:

¶ Sade's gigantomachies of sex are not to be dismissed as the hallucinations of a sick brain. The word "obscene" simply does not apply. What is going on here is not seduction but the discovery of ghastly things. . . . Sade belongs not to the rococo age but to the era of the unleashing of the forces of nature. . . . Anyone who compares a series of life histories from the time of the Ancien Régime with the characters in his novels will recognize that Sade is no visionary. Sade ran the gamut of the situations of debauchery, particularly rape, brutality, and the ambivalence of executioner and victim. Shortly before this Choderlos de Laclos had drawn a brilliant picture of calculatingly provocative resistance. He had already ranked the desire to dominate above sensual pleasure in importance and discovered a motive for rape, brutality, and destruction in a desire to avenge humiliations inflicted upon their perpetrator. Sade exposed a still deeper stratum. . . . Sade discovered the lostness of the eternally isolated body and revealed its isolation precisely at the point where it becomes dualistic (or, in the case of promiscuity, even pluralistic). The very act of embrace reveals the impossibility of ever reaching one another. The orgy becomes superlative emptiness.

¶ It is easy to reduce this idea to sociological terms. In a significant interpretation of Sade, Mme de Beauvoir says that the brothel, public or private, was the last remaining area where the feudal lords of the Ancien Régime, now deprived of power, could still be tyrants. Seen in this light, these orgies were nothing but stage settings in the spectacle of an expiring *"l'État, c'est moi."*[5]

These are suggestive analyses of the convertibility of male aggressiveness. Marcuse sees Sade as a utopian whose images anticipated future events, though twentieth-century realities, such as saturation bombing, genocide, and extermination camps, far outstrip Sade's imagination.

In terms of our present thesis, this means that the progressive divorce of sexuality from traditional moral forms does not in itself lead to genuine liberation. It is just as likely to produce new constraint: namely, a compulsion to bestialize humanity. The sex wave and its accentuation of the battle of the sexes is proof enough of this point. Despite the spread of enlightenment (which progresses almost automatically, thanks to the mass media), we are well on the way to a monstrous distortion of consciousness, to a new false consciousness. Sexuality is being increasingly perverted and alienated as extraneous factors are superimposed upon it. A disturbing symptom is the fact that it is now possible nearly everywhere to conscript women for military service without encountering the least resistance; another is women's increasing participation in extremely hazardous competitive sports. Contraceptive know-how and the attendant control over her own body gives a woman a kind of freedom formerly enjoyed only by men. Like them, she can now channel activism and aggression into the sexual sphere, and possesses an unprecedented freedom to use sex as a weapon, so that sex becomes at least potentially a violent, ruthless form of mutual aggression.

These are, of course, only extreme possibilities. Most people tend to remain amazingly normal and balanced, managing their private relationships with considerable individuality. But to do so they must resist increasing pressures and must learn to cope with conflict as never before. It takes a great deal of David Riesman's tradition-directedness or inner-directedness—which are disappearing virtues, according to him—to maintain one's balance in the face of incessant mechanical, propagandistic appeals to sexuality which, after hunger and the instinct for pure motor activity, is the most powerful and elemental of human drives. The contemporary consciousness is saturated with an artificially stimulated fascination with the pursuit of sexual pleasure for its own sake, as an end in itself.

A definitive symptom of this overvaluation of sex is the interest the public takes in sex crimes—which, the experts tell us, are steadily on the increase. The psychopathology of the criminal is not the only cause of such crimes; there is no doubt that the social climate contains aggravating factors. One of the most important of these is the extraordinary overtaxing and consequent frustration of sexuality in general, and in a variety of common psychosexual disorders.

These disorders often breed extreme violence, disastrous aberrations. The ability to face and control one's own hidden nature is given to few; for most, a sudden burst of vitality, an unlucky turn of events, may be enough to precipitate crime. Objectively, it will be a Freudian error of conduct, a misdirected effort to adjust. If popular fiction and news stories constantly challenge a man to commit seduction, rape, and brutality of every kind, it is no wonder that, given a uniform in the service of a war machine, he becomes capable of committing any atrocity.

Schelsky has shown that only in a society which "persistently 'abnormalizes' itself structurally and hence has largely abrogated or lost its normative, institutional force" do we find a direct road leading from the psychology of the abnormal to the sociology of the normal.[6] This seems to apply to the society of our time. Thus our universal official condemnation of certain sexual anomalies, particularly those caused by compensated aggression, is not without a certain ambiguity. We have a double moral standard: the standard of the courtroom, the official moral code we loudly profess, and the standard of the mass media and our winking connivance in their exploitation of the sadism and brutality latent in society.

Two sexual perversions in particular hold such fascination for the public that one begins to suspect they are no more than extreme cases of the aggression-charged sexual behavior which by now almost qualifies as "normal." The first of these is what I shall call the "Moosbrugger complex," after a character in Robert Musil's great novel about Western culture in decline, *The Man Without Qualities.* This book, which is actually a parable about male qualities that are losing their meaning in modern society, places the mad rapist-killer Moosbrugger at the center of the action. The illiterate, inarticulate Moosbrugger contrasts strangely with the other main characters, who are supersensitive and pampered Viennese of the upper class in the period before the outbreak of World War I.

The story of *The Man Without Qualities* concerns a society which, notwithstanding all its conscious efforts, is forced by historical circumstances into a situation which renders it incapable of action, so that its show of maintaining its functions becomes a kind of play-acting. The people who, as citizens and public servants, would normally exercise those political and economic functions can now only go through the motions. Their love affairs must provide them with a feeling of reality, a sense of having a social existence, a stability that has disappeared from social and political life.

In a series of erotic configurations apexed by the mystically heightened cohabitation of a brother and sister, Musil goes through the whole catalog of basic love relationships, examining their durability and finding it wanting. The social world he is analyzing keeps falling apart. As the Habsburg Empire, in which all faith has been lost, disintegrates, the erotic bases of all human brotherhood atrophy. In this world not a single marriage remains intact and unthreatened; none of the love affairs is happy. The amorous encounters Musil describes, even if they last only as long as it takes to consummate them, never bring even a fleeting sense of union, but only destruction or the awareness of unbridgeable distance between the lovers.

In this collapsing society there exists a single common element which, although the characters do not realize it, substitutes in some way for their lost sense of community. This is the dreadful fascination exerted by a sex criminal at large, the whore killer Moosbrugger. All the characters in the novel, from servant girls and the man in the street to artists, industrial magnates, and top politicians, take sides in the case and are preoccupied, in a way which they themselves could never define, with Moosbrugger's crimes and his fate. It is not really a question of whether he is sane or insane (and hence guilty or not guilty). What matters to this deactivated society, whose endless talk, far from producing a fresh orientation, merely aggravates its disorientation, is the activist quality of these crimes. Moosbrugger represents the eruption of a primitive, mysterious imperative into a world where everything else is no more than possibility. To a society so incapable of action, a society which stumbled into a world war only because of external circumstances, a brute able to take action at will must look almost like a redeemer.

Moosbrugger, the incongruous exemplar of male aggression, activism degenerated to violence by a lack of purpose, turns out to be as much a central character as Ulrich, the "man without qualities," the upper-class intellectual who is the novel's chief protagonist. Where Moosbrugger is dehumanized because his natural masculinity has gone brutally astray, Ulrich is dehumanized because he has refined himself out of all capacity for decision and action. There is a suggestion here of the science fiction alternative predicted in the words of Gottfried Benn: "The coming century will put the masculine world in a vise, confront it with a decision from which there can be no escape, no emigration. It will admit only two types of men, two constitutions, two ways of reacting: those who act and want

to get ahead, and those who silently await the transformation, the historical men, and the deep ones, criminals and
monks."[7] The increase in number of the monks has not
kept pace with that of the criminals, unfortunately.

I am not sure whether Musil recognized Moosbrugger's extraordinary kinship with Hitler; Musil began the
novel in 1918 and continued writing it until his death in
1942. But from the contemporary perspective there can be
no doubt that a deep inner connection exists between a
society's fascination with the primitive, perverse bestiality
of such criminals and a society's fascination with political
leaders who organize bestiality on a large scale.* The cult
of the leader in our day is variously interpreted as an expression of the longing for a lost father image and the like.
Yet beneath the idealistic surface lurk the effects of libidinal
repressions, the distortions of natural drives made homeless
or illegitimate by the vagaries of history. A startling instance is an incident during the Russian troops' victory
rampage in East Germany in 1945, when Ilya Ehrenburg,
a leader in Stalin's cultural establishment, incited the Russian soldiers to rape with the slogan: "Break the German
women's pride." The frank offer of the defeated enemy's
women as a safety valve to the ravening troops here wears
only the most transparent veil of ideology.

* As Musil's diaries show, his attitude toward Hitler fluctuated. He calls
him "a passion incarnate" (*Tagebücher* [Hamburg; 1955], p. 358), yet
cannot entirely resist his fascination. Musil, who emigrated to Switzerland,
sees Hitler both as the greatest criminal and "the great historical figure"
(p. 527).

Participation in political parties or mass movements or wars aiming at total destruction of the opponent is only a symptom of the same social perversion which in more quiescent times expresses itself in criminals of the Moosbrugger type and their voyeuristic following. The criminal and his public, the führer and his mass following, are in league with one another, though in the first case the link is more concealed. In both instances the latent perversion in the masses encourages, provokes, sometimes even precipitates, crime. Moosbrugger thinks of his public, is flattered by its interest, and considers his actions legitimized by it, as innumerable psychopaths of the Bonnie-and-Clyde sort have always done. Seen in this light, he is nothing but a member of the public who actualizes some of its own latent possibilities, for which "service" he is also a scapegoat after he is caught. As a member of the public he abandons the role of spectator or voyeur for that of the actor on center stage, whose function is to reassert the dignity of the natural, aggressive, action-taking male. Nearly all criminals of this type tend to behave in an extraordinarily theatrical manner in court, more like actors in a cheap melodrama than defendants in a criminal case. Freud's thesis* that we borrow psychic energies from our sexual life to produce our culture turns out to be reversible: pent-up activism

---

* "Since man has not an unlimited amount of mental energy at his disposal, he must accomplish his tasks by distributing his libido to the best advantage. What he employs for cultural purposes he withdraws to a great extent from women and his sexual life." Sigmund Freud: *Civilization and Its Discontents* (London: Hogarth Press; 1939), p. 73.

70

and aggression, deprived of other outlets, may seek one in sex, so much of which has become commercialized and perverted. This is what breeds the Moosbruggers among us, and fosters the Moosbrugger complex in our society.

An actual Moosbrugger is, of course, always an extreme case, an enigma. The crimes of a Charles J. Whitman,* a Richard Speck,† a Boston Strangler can occur anywhere and at any time, though today more of them seem to be occurring more often than ever before. They have almost come to be a part of our daily lives—tidbits for the popular newspapers and mass-circulation magazines, banquets for the yellow press which we have always with us. *Christ in der Zeit,* the German weekly, published an article on this subject entitled "Mass Applause for Murder."[8] A being from another planet unfamiliar with the complicated structure of our society might take such incidents as cultic events staged for the mass media.

Another grave perversion of male consciousness in our time might be called the "Lolita complex" after Vladimir Nabokov's novel *Lolita,* which deals with a love affair between a man of forty and a twelve-year-old girl. While most critics agree that the book has great literary merit, its tremendous success owed more to its shock value than to its aesthetic quality. "*Lolita*," said one commentator, "more

---

* In the summer of 1966 Charles Joseph Whitman, after murdering his mother and his wife, fired into the crowd from a tower on the University of Texas campus; twelve people were killed and thirty-one wounded.
† Richard Speck forced his way into a nurses' home in Chicago and raped and murdered eight nurses.

or less disposes of the last remaining social taboo in the
erotic sphere: the sexual untouchability of girls who are
still children."[9] Humbert Humbert, the weirdly named
protagonist, marries Lolita's mother to gain control over
the child. When the mother conveniently dies, he lives with
the girl, keeping her more or less captive by traveling
around the country with her until she runs off with another
man who promises her a film career.

Because of its subject matter, the book might have
been expected to arouse the kind of indignation that erupts
whenever a child actually has been sexually assaulted. No
such thing happened; it was greeted, quite rightly, with
critical admiration as excellent social satire and a work of
high art. Nevertheless, its subject matter does represent an
item in criminal statistics, in view of the steadily increasing
incidence of sexual assaults on children. Nabokov, having
all sorts of other fish to fry, merely presented the perversion
so brilliantly and in such a sympathetic light that the reader
forgets his natural indignation. As Lionel Trilling said, we
are all the more indignant when we realize that in the
course of reading the book we have come to forgive the
crime it presents. Trilling has an ingenious explanation for
this: In our sober, conformist society, he suggests, passionate love, an almost pathological kind of suffering celebrated
in European literature since the Minnesingers, is no longer
plausible. It has been ousted by an "enlightened" modern,
especially American, love ideal of the mutually tolerant,
stable, happy marriage partnership of equals. To present
absolute, enslaving love convincingly today, Nabokov

seems to be saying, you have to use some form of hopeless perversion (in the bourgeois sense). *Lolita*, according to Trilling, is not about sex, though it may be present on every page, but about love.

But we cannot properly appreciate the book's long-range effects or those of the movie made from it if we disregard the fundamental fact of the sexual crime. The close analysis of Nabokov's magically cryptic world view, and the placement of the novel in the hierarchy of world literature, are of interest to an elite. The general public finds *Lolita*'s literary profundities rather a nuisance and contents itself with the surface, as the movie does too: that is, with the simple fact of a mature male's passionate desire for a child-woman, for a girl on the brink of womanhood. To put it crudely, fresh blood and youthful flesh have always been prized in the male world. (In the book Nabokov lists instances from many different civilizations.) The age at which a young girl is no longer taboo to the male varies considerably from culture to culture; even today there are countries where Humbert Humbert's conduct would not be considered criminal. And while it does not justify his actions, the fact is that his "nymphet" is not really a child any more; she is described as a precocious, artful little female, who has already traded her virginity for some experience at a summer camp. Nabokov's satire on the mores of contemporary teenagers, at this point, attacks conditions not peculiar to America.

Behind all this we detect one of our culture's acute problems: In the male world of today a preference for very

young girls—the younger the better—is by no means un-
usual. Broadly speaking, our society is given to a curious
cult of young girls. A glance at the dominant female image
upheld by our mass media shows that it is based chiefly on
juvenile models of femininity. The girl in the miniskirt is
a juvenile. By way of comparison, the feminine ideal of
the baroque era took as its model the mature, motherly
woman, beginning as early as da Vinci's Mona Lisa. Even
the youngest of Ruben's women, the seventeen-year-old
Helene Fourment, who was his second wife, or Rem-
brandt's Hendrickje Stoffels, are stylized images of the
fully mature woman. In contrast, we have Twiggy, baby-
faced, flat-chested, bony-legged—an ambiguous girl-boy
permanently under twenty years old.

The idealization of the pubescent girl forces the
grown woman to style herself as a girl-child, with occasionally grotesque effects. The actual juveniles, as a result, are
encouraged to enter sexual competition at an increasingly
early age. The precocious sexualization and accelerated
maturation produced by the sex wave makes many girls
sexually provocative long before the legal age of consent—
a taboo line most civilizations try to maintain, against increasing odds. One might even say that Lolitas are created
by overwhelming social pressures, and are in that sense
victims of society rather than little daemons like Nabokov's
prototype.

Thus the Lolita complex is only a component in the
wrong that male society has done women by having failed
her. This failure is a logical consequence of the total com-

mercialization of sex. The search for ever-new forms of sex stimuli not yet discovered by the market must automatically turn to something new, to the rising generation of girls just coming into bloom. Sex propaganda does not emphasize the appeal of older generations, as advertisements for cognac or wine do, but relies on the same "superfresh merchandise" line that sells vegetables, fruit, and meat; in this context sex is only an "organically grown" natural comestible. *Lolita* is a literary representation of a common, not to say banal reality. In this reality pubescent girls are sold off by their families to seventy-year-old millionaires; an elderly film producer tells journalists that girls over eighteen no longer interest him; movie stars marry girls younger than their own daughters from previous marriages, enjoy them for a time, and then get a divorce and begin all over again. Lillian Hellman, in her autobiography *An Unfinished Woman*, tells of a Russian mother quite frankly bringing her pubescent daughter to a high Soviet official as an article for consumption. Such a taste for "fresh meat" is by no means confined to the decadent West.

In essence the Lolita complex denotes man's boredom with women of his own age, of his own generation; it is a sign of his retreat from woman as a life companion. She is superseded by the incessantly advertised, idealized image of the girlish playmate, the eternal glamour girl, whose very nature precludes growing old and who must therefore be exchanged at regular intervals for the latest model. Even though this is not feasible in practice for many men, the sex wave promotes the tendency. Hence we see many men who for various reasons preserve their marriages outwardly intact but keep younger mistresses. For the other-directed man, a young girlfriend has become almost as much of a status symbol as a well-stocked home bar or a high-powered sports car.

This function of sex as a status symbol represents a sort of official agreement arrived at by the masculine world. The false consciousness produced by commercially manipulated sex produces its own image of masculinity, one feature of which is *conspicuous sex consumption.* The way to "make it" is to date, conspicuously, the most sought-after girls. David Riesman's characterization of sex as "the last frontier" is justified from two points of view: first, sex represents the attainment of pleasure in individual isolation, and second, it confirms one's social standing or serves as a substitute for it. For many men, sexual success intensifies their triumphs in the struggle for territory or status; for other men, who are breaking into the sexual territories of those on top, it is a substitute for their lack of social standing. The erotic aspect is of little importance. True Eros needs no publicity—even shuns it. An essential characteristic of genuine eroticism is that it exists for its own sake; whether others know about it or not is immaterial. Indeed, its greatest triumph is that it can do entirely without all "fringe benefits" such as personal advantage, material profit, social recognition, or envy, because it is self-sufficient and self-confirming. What we see today is not so much Eros as people playing with the language of Eros,

76

even though the game often takes the form of an attempt to find and recapture the lost Eros.

Thus many a man, trying to break out of the institutionalized communion of a marriage which is burdened with economic and social obligations and which may also have been overtaxing him sexually, will seek self-renewal in sexual adventures without being at all aware of how strongly he is propelled by artificial stimuli. But the magical, fresh, unpremeditated erotic encounter with the girl goddess of his dreams generally turns out to be a coldly prefabricated illusion. The actual girl goddesses love the men who can afford them, for as long as they can afford them and their special kind of expensive display; the relationships border on prostitution, weighted down as they are by the enchanting creature's incessant demands for gifts and money or else by her maneuvers for advantages, career opportunities, social advancement. Humbert Humbert is bitterly disillusioned when his nymphet leaves him for a higher bidder. That she eventually settles for the domesticity of a drab marriage with a commonplace young man only proves that she was merely a precociously sexualized but otherwise quite normal female: the divine nymph, the child goddess, is a masculine fantasy based on a romantic misconception. The need to escape from a wife with whom one has to discuss grocery bills while paying personal bills without question may lead a man to form a relationship in which he must prove his generosity in ways that are even more costly and more effectively enslaving. Men can neither buy nor manipulate what women most deeply want from them: the repetition of an elemental event of great emotional power, the tender magic of having their capacity for love awakened and aroused to an infinite outpouring, an ecstatic escape from self. The inexperienced, curious, naïve girlishness that so powerfully attracts mature men does not last. In real life, the little nymph undergoes an all too rapid metamorphosis—at best into a normal mature woman, although the sex wave increases her chances of turning into a neurotic nymphomaniac or a professional one.

In a world intent upon its technological advances, Eros too undergoes technification. Sex propaganda, sex marketing techniques, lead to a brutal and perverse kind of pan-sexualization. It is the male world which is behind all this, promoting a stylization of the male sexual role inspired by sidetracked aggression. The female complement to this role is a vacuous idol, a lifelike sex doll, an eternal party girl —a role no human female can fill for long, though many try.

Another perversion encouraged by contemporary social conditions and unrestrained sexualization is homosexuality, considered by experts to be the most common sexual anomaly. According to the Kinsey Report, half the male population of the United States has at some period of life followed homosexual tendencies in some form, and authorities believe that these findings apply to most societies in modern Western civilization. Only a small proportion of all homosexuals (4 per cent of the total male population) are considered exclusively homosexual; 46 per cent have indulged in more or less active hetero- and homosexual activity. According to Kinsey, the number of homosexual women is much smaller: approximately one third of the above figures.

The general public's vigorous censure of homosexuality does not reflect how widespread it is. The English sociologist Geoffrey Gorer explains the hysterical fear of homosexuality by the fact that most men feel themselves directly threatened by it. Fear of homosexual seduction is so great in the United States that homosexuals are not accepted for military service. That the fear is also present in Europe, though in a weaker form, is attested by the fact that homosexuality has been a prosecutable offense in most countries.

What is the reason for this fear? Why do we not draw the logical conclusion from the fact that half the male population is susceptible to homosexuality? Why prohibit it? These questions are now being asked more and more frequently in public discussions as people point to the findings of sex research and advocate reform of the criminal law. The problems of homosexuality are also being analyzed: recent years have brought a whole series of homosexual plays, such as Charles Dyer's *Staircase*, John Osborne's *A Patriot for Me*, and Frank Marcus's *The Killing of Sister George*. Centuries of sexual taboos in European culture are being rapidly broken down. The general wave of propaganda for absolute sexual freedom brings with it an increasingly vociferous demand for the sanctioning of homosexuality, and substantial reforms of the laws against homosexuals have recently been enacted in Britain and Germany.

But liberal trends in sex education and recommendations that homosexuality be tolerated may serve to propagandize this perversion, even to make it fashionable. Its presence or absence in a society, or at least its conspicuousness, is largely determined by prevalent social attitudes. Among the Greeks, particularly the Spartans, it was firmly anchored in the culture, for there pederasty served the interests of militarism. In that male-dominated society, where children were taken from their mothers at the age of seven, education consisted almost entirely of preparation for military service. Men lived not with their families but in tent communities, eating, sleeping, and exercising together. The male sex was considered the beautiful sex. An adolescent who did not find favor with an older lover was derided as being "left on the shelf." Even so-called Platonic love, far from being "Platonic" in our sense, was a philosophical idealization of sexual relationships between men. The fact that such cultural stylizations can occur and remain predominant for centuries shows the great variability and flexibility of man's sexual nature.

Many post-Freudian sexologists assume that man is actually bisexual by nature. Freud himself said that the human infant is "polymorphously perverse," in that he finds erotic stimulation in everything. This is, to be sure, an extreme view not shared by all sexologists. Kretschmer, for instance, believes that there is homosexuality which is biological in origin. Here a hermaphroditic glandular tendency produces more or less pronounced characteristics of the opposite sex, and the psychic attitude is determined by the psychological effects of hormone activity. Such cases of true congenital homosexuality, of what might be called "nature's mistakes," are relatively rare. The vast majority of cases are thought to be psychogenic in origin and stem from environmental influences. In our culture, in which no institutionalized, legally sanctioned form of this perversion exists, homosexuality is usually due to a false orientation at an early stage of sexual maturation. The pubescent boy first experiences the sex instinct as a vague, still undifferentiated impulse. Being self-centered, it tends toward self-gratification. Since the adolescent's social life is often predominantly with members of his own sex, this autistic gratification is readily extended to include his friends. Often older boys play the role of seducer. These preliminary stages of homosexuality generally begin with collective masturbation and later lead into homosexual practices. The surprisingly high percentage of occasional homosexuals noted by Kinsey is largely accounted for by early adolescent episodes of this kind, which are almost routine in boarding schools, juvenile homes, and summer camps. If they are counteracted soon enough by experiences with the opposite sex, educational challenges, and a maturing judgment, they remain merely episodic, and there is no fixation of the perversion. But if homosexuality persists, we can speak of what Margaret Mead calls a learning defect.

This learning defect is now spreading to include all of society. The necessary conditions have been created by the collapse of the traditional male role, which has been undermined by the findings of sexology itself and by changed social circumstances. All-out sex propaganda and the fashionable cry for absolute sexual freedom have a destabilizing effect and lead to a demand that all variations from the norm be tolerated. The logic of this demand is undeniable; where everything seems "naturally" possible, everything ought to be permissible.

Of course, many sexologists have greatly exaggerated the "bisexual tendency" of human nature because they have derived most of their knowledge from pathological cases. If we consider the social factors that codetermine modes of masculine and feminine sexual behavior, we arrive at quite different results. One factor that is often of decisive importance is the social segregation, almost compulsory in Europe, of pubescent boys. A similar situation occurs among adults in jails, prison camps, and many special groups restricted to men, such as the military services or isolated work camps. If the imprinting of the heterosexual role has been inadequate, there may be a regression to adolescent habits and hence to homosexual practices. Another contributing social factor is what Schelsky calls "the casting off of normative inhibitions." This, he says, is most evident in criminals in whom "asocial modes of behavior . . . begin to affect sexual habits." He believes that all social isolation and also the emergence of minorities that are oppositional in principle lead to similar effects. "Thus among the strongly antisocial avant-garde protest groups of young intellectuals, especially those with literary overtones, we find a higher than average incidence of homosexual relationships."[10] A third factor triggering the release of inhibitions is the collapse of the social order as a result of economic disasters or revolutions. In Schelsky's opinion it is not just a conservative prejudice to see a connection between revolution and immorality.

But the fourth factor mentioned by Schelsky seems to me the decisive one. Citing Abram Kardiner, he blames the structure of modern industrial society itself for the fact that a "flight from masculinity" is now occurring in the sexual role." Unlike the other factors we have discussed, this is not a matter of isolation from women or a general lowering of norms, but of a bypassing of the male sexual role as a result of social conditions. Kardiner thinks there is less opportunity for masculinity today. The ever more taxing demands upon men in professional life and the ruthless competition make it more and more difficult for men to assert their masculinity successfully. He stresses the fact that woman is steadily increasing her consumer demands and at the same time competing with man in professional life. In this situation many men feel inadequate in their sexual role and therefore assume a protection-seeking attitude in their sexual behavior. The requirements of competition and success have made the obligation to be masculine burdensome to this type of man. He can expect no comfort or support from women because he sees them as a threat; no consolation, because they expect him to be manly.

This produces a "fear of the female" quite different from the fear which psychoanalysis deduced from clinical case histories and labeled the Oedipus complex. What we have here is a fear of the masculine role, a role which the climate of the managerial industrial society is rendering increasingly absurd and which for that very reason is presented by the illusionist mass media in ever more outrageously unrealistic idealizations. Actually, male and female roles are constantly being brought closer together by the conditions of industrial life. As Schelsky says:

¶ The increasing sexual neutrality of our working conditions and our public and cultural life, which results only partially from the social emancipation of women but primarily from the development of our technological and organizational production structure—this depersonalizing materialization and functionalization of our modern way of life makes a standard of male behavior that is to be binding for all men and attainable by all men increasingly amorphous and uncertain. "Masculinity" is deflected into ever more arbitrary and subjective areas of personality formation and loses its social significance in our society.[12]

Arnold Gehlen draws attention to another aspect of this process. He describes the development of a passive consumer mentality in the male as "a kind of feminization" on the grounds that "heretofore at least the whole business of consumption, especially luxury consumption, carried on without reservations or qualms of conscience, has been a privilege of women." Gehlen cites Riesman's thesis that inner-directed behavior is dying out: "That is to say, we now rarely see men who act according to personal, inner values and 'on principles' which permit them to maintain their general stance regardless of fortuitous situational changes."[13]

As Alexander Mitscherlich has shown, this behavioral uncertainty can also be ascribed to the collapse of the father image. Mitscherlich outlines the psychoanalytic view of the origin of homosexuality as follows: "Thus the paternalistic symbol of authority as we know it decisively influences the form which the sexual identity takes as the bisexual tendencies recede. If the father image collapses . . . this is bound to create a libidinal unrest extending far beyond the consciousness. Loss of the father orientation destroys the security in his role which man previously took entirely for granted."[14] Even if the psychoanalytic interpretation cannot claim to be the only valid one, since a number of other social causes contribute to the occurrence of psychogenic homosexuality, the loss of the father image as a social fact plays a major part. This is the situation in all cases of homosexuality with which I am familiar; in no case have I ever found a dominant, feared father, but always a weakening of the father image to the point of actual loss. Only where the father image is totally distorted can the general feminizing tendency, interacting with a sex education which is misinterpreted as propaganda for complete sexual freedom, produce what might be called "fashionable" homosexuality.

This is a real danger today for the members of our younger generation who are committed to the absurdist rebellion against society. Their striving for absolute freedom, the lack of any reliable training for the traditional male role, the feminine stylization they deliberately adopt as a positive gesture of antimilitarism, and their artificially created position as social outsiders, all combine to push them in this direction. Nor should we overlook the fact that the slum conditions in which these rebels choose to live and their propensity for inhibition-releasing drugs bring many of them into conflict with the law, so that they become *de facto* criminals. In this way the idealistic "reappraisal of values" to which they aspire may easily lead to the total loss of all ethical norms. A particularly significant point is that in these groups, especially in the most extreme of them, girls and women are a disappearing minority. Under the law of complete sexual freedom the logical result is promiscuity and homosexuality.

Because of its origin, because it stems from the bypassing of the sexual partner, homosexuality is never far removed from an infantile autistic, self-centered libido. Unless some institutionalizing cultural form exists to support it, homosexuality possesses little potential for personal maturation or the growth of mutual responsibility. It is not conducive to the heightening of love into the shared self-understanding, the kind of *tertium comparationis*, that is a natural and fundamental feature of love between man and woman, if only because of its capacity to fulfill the biological function of reproduction. It is this tendency to infantilism, rather than any social censure of homosexuals, which is the reason why homosexual relationships are nearly always temporary and casual. Their basically autistic character permits no deepening or broadening of emotional relations; on the contrary, these relations tend to be impoverished and to atrophy. Homosexuality is fundamentally antisocial. It can achieve social value only in purely military societies, as in Sparta, a state keyed to fighting and war. Only in such a culture can homosexuality become institutionally anchored, in the sense that Plato had in mind when he wrote in the *Republic:* "If it were possible for a whole state or a whole army camp to consist of lovers and their favorites, no better community could possibly be imagined, because out of consideration for one another they would abstain from everything bad and continually vie with each other in noble competition. When it came to battle they would triumph over every adversary even if they were outnumbered. For a lover would rather the whole world should see him running away than that his beloved should." By its very nature, homosexuality can attain no social function other than improving performance in aggressive male societies.

Hence there is a fundamental fallacy in the psychotherapeutic idea that it is better to act out than to suppress latent homosexuality in order to prevent it from turning into aggression and political sadism. In reality, official sanction and tolerance of homosexuality would inevitably lead to official tolerance of homosexual cliques, which would necessarily establish themselves within all-male societies such as terrorist groups and military organizations, where they would pursue aggressive ends. Thus the flight from woman which predominates in "fashionable" homosexuality is suspect on social grounds.

The retreat from maturity which is embodied in sexual perversions is also manifested in a growing use of intoxicants.

In addition to the alcoholic beverages that have long been common (though never before consumed on the scale which they are today), many new drugs are being used. It is notable that they are not employed, as alcohol is, for the sake of their stimulating or inhibition-releasing effect, but for a completely different purpose: to produce dream states and semi-trances involving purely subjective experiences. The aim is basically to escape into an inner world, an artificially induced dream kingdom. The most commonly used drugs are hallucinogens such as the now notorious LSD and the old stand-by hashish, whose better-known relative is marijuana. Since these drugs have the property of creating an artificial consciousness and evoking hallucinatory images out of man's own psyche, they have been called "consciousness-expanding" drugs, and some kind of power to induce religious experiences has been ascribed to them. Gottfried Benn said long ago that God is a drug, and this has been reiterated by prophets of the artificially induced consciousness such as Aldous Huxley and Dr. Timothy Leary, who was dismissed from Harvard in 1963 for experimenting with narcotics in his seminar. Dr. Leary, who argues that the narcotics he uses are less injurious than alcohol or nicotine, has founded a sect, supported by private contributions, which uses narcotics for "religious inspiration." He also does a great deal of lecturing, advocating the legalization of narcotics.

Independently of these prophets, a trend toward drug taking has long been developing among young people in America and has now extended to certain sections of European youth. Pop musicians and beat philosophers were the first to start dropping out of reality occasionally and seeking escape in dream worlds. Whether or not the younger generation began by following their example, we can assume that the general climate of our time is ultimately responsible for this proclivity for drugs. Apart from the hallucinogens, a number of other drugs regularly prescribed for medical purposes—all kinds of stimulants, stay-awake and sleeping pills, and tranquilizers—are being taken, often by school children. Young drug users also favor such products as acetone-based glue, spot removers, and codeine-containing cough syrups. What the consumers of these "beginners' drugs" are after is not at all the same as what alcohol users are seeking. Only in its most acute forms does alcoholism produce delusions, and then they are an unintended side effect. Young drug takers regard alcoholism as the vice of old fogies, members of an outdated generation, for the young want something more than stimulation. Apart from "accidents" caused by habituation or overdoses, the idea is to produce visions and delusions in order to endow reality with new imaginative content. What they are aiming at is trance, self-transcendence, and remythologization.

Even if drug use is often accompanied by a desire to try out possible new modes of behavior for a masculine role appropriate to contemporary conditions, the escape element remains unmistakable. It is a flight from reality, from the deepening of sex, and from an Eros which creates human ties and seeks responsibility. I believe that a growing dependence on narcotics indicates disorders which also affect the erotic sphere, some of which in fact originate there. These too can be regarded as symptoms of an emasculated age. It makes little difference whether the drugs are taken as stimulants or narcotics; their use represents a frantic search for a way out on the part of a despairing masculinity which has learned to accept the idea that it is entitled to unrestricted pleasure and yet cannot manage to conform to the specious models it is supposed to emulate.

Obviously, youth will try to escape from any situation it finds intolerable and in doing so will be vulnerable to the seductions it encounters. Youth is always more ready to experiment than age—and hence is always exposed to greater dangers. It is also more apt to indulge in self-deception; where the young see themselves as the avant-garde, they may in fact be only the victims of circumstance. They may believe they are inventing a new life style when they are actually succumbing to the propaganda of the mass media.

The effect on youth of the unbridled sex wave is the teenage eroticism which exists today. Civilized societies where the educational process is prolonged probably always have a juvenile sexual problem of some kind, and the stricter the ban on premarital relations, the greater the problem will be. This was the case until fairly recently. Erotic relations between young people had to be clandestine, carried on in constant fear of discovery, often burdened with shame and guilt. While this was obviously not a desirable state of affairs, it did have one advantage: the juvenile sexual problem was not constantly exacerbated by a hothouse sexual atmosphere. Today, sexualization is not the direct result of biological maturation; it is promoted, even in little children, by provocative sex propaganda. Children in our time already have what Riesman calls an "other-directed knowledge of sex" which may be very troubling to them. Comparing the effects of sex education in tradition-directed and other-directed societies, Riesman makes some acute observations. In the tradition-directed society, he says,

¶ The child, knowledgeable for example about sex, could see reflections of it in the daily adult life around him. He would know that if his uncle was particularly gay or particularly cross at work this was connected with what happened in the village the night before. As against this, the other-directed child knows about sex only, so to speak, in the abstract. He cannot reasonably connect the night life he knows exists with the seriousness of the adult world that faces him at school, at the store, or at home. While he has doffed the myths of sex that Freud found among the young of his day, he still finds passion playing a greater role in the comics and the movies than in the life he is able to observe—the latter being a life in which people are trained to hide their passions and to act generally in a disembodied way. Perhaps this is one reason why sex often remains an exciting mystery for the other-directed adult.[15]

The extravagant overvaluation of sex can, it appears, be implanted in earliest childhood through other-directed

knowledge of the subject, perhaps even more effectively
than through personal experience. Think of the Barbie dolls
with their bosoms and high-fashion clothes, which are already helping to shape little girls' dreams of what they
themselves will be like tomorrow. Think of the "little
brother doll" complete with all accouterments, including a
penis guaranteed to stand handling. Think of mass-circulation teenager magazines which concentrate entirely on subliminal sexualization. A direct consequence is the noticeable
increase in public necking and kissing: never before has
there been so much overt embracing and hand holding. This
trend has reached a climax in school "kiss-ins" and in demands that the pill be made available to schoolgirls. One is
tempted to regard these phenomena, along with the ecstatic
carryings-on at rock concerts and dances, as signs of a worldwide sexual hysteria among young people.

But the juvenile sex problem is much more complicated in its motivation than the individual symptoms suggest. Sexuality continues to press its libidinal claims, as it
always has, stimulated and fomented as never before. But
instead of being restrained by traditional norms, some of
them intact, some modified, these claims now have a number
of extraneous desires superimposed upon them. A typical
example is petting, the principal juvenile sexual diversion,
defined by Margaret Mead as "a variety of sexual practices
that will not result in pregnancy." While petting may include most normal erotic activities, it is more of a social
game than a genuine form of sexual behavior. Affectionate
or passionate erotic relations have almost no part in it; the

main thing is to prove one's sex appeal and desirability. Here love actually becomes a kind of party game. In petting much more importance is attached to getting plenty of dates and thus ensuring one's popularity than to sexual pleasure. To quote Margaret Mead:

¶ Children are drawn into the dating game not by their bodies, but by their assertiveness, their desire to achieve, to succeed, to be popular. Yet the game is cast in highly sexual terms. . . . Viewed from the standpoint of another culture, . . . this all gives a picture of a people, especially a youth group, who are tremendously preoccupied with sex, whose only interest in life is love, and whose definition of love is purely physical. Yet this seems to me to be an enormous misstatement. Rather, this continuous emphasis on the sexually relevant physical appearance is an outcome of using a heterosexual game as the prototype for success and popularity in adolescence.[16]

Although this was written with American conditions in mind, it is becoming more and more applicable to affluent industrial society anywhere. Such a practice shatters the complexity of the erotic experience into pieces which to the consciousness appear completely isolated. Biological function, pleasure, and emotional experience are subordinated to the pursuit of social status. Here again we see the extent to which sex has been commercialized.

Sexual practices among the young who are involved

in the absurdist rebellion also demonstrate the projection of social aspirations into sex. Here, however, the projection takes a different form, since their claim to complete sexual freedom rejects petting as a bourgeois custom. This rebellion may at first suggest a revised edition of "Sexpol," a politicosexual movement of the late 1920's based on a Russian model, which attempted to combine psychoanalysis and Marxism in a single theory. But, in fact, the young rebels' claim to an unrestricted sex life is heavily loaded with unrecognized or misunderstood social urges which have been superimposed on it. As we have seen, principles of male territorial fighting are being transposed to sex, which is becoming a kind of territory substitute for social outsiders. In the absurdist rebellion, sex is being perverted in a curious collective manner by groups of young men. Something that deserves particular attention is the announcement, incessantly proclaimed by beat philosophers and hippie ideologists, of full sexual freedom for women. Strangely enough, though, they always speak of a combination of one woman and several men, never the other way around. (The student leader Rudi Dutschke, among others, has advocated this sort of sexual grouping.) But such an arrangement, while claiming to represent total freedom for women, simply places one girl at the disposal of a group of men and ultimately tends to degrade women. Behind it can be detected a homosexually oriented morality, like that of some military societies, which does not want any inward or responsible bond between man and woman. What pretends to be a new sexual morality is actually a betrayal of woman by man.

The new sexual morality is a ludicrous mixture of various perversions. Here autism, homosexual tendencies, and impotent voyeurism enter into a kind of symbiosis.* Thus in the world of today, sex enlightenment can lead to abuse. The findings of sex research can have a seductive influence, especially on the premature proclamations of sex prophets who turn variations from the norm into normality because they derive their concept of normality from their experience with clinical cases. This can lead to a confusion which may be more injurious than the old sexual morality with its unequivocal censure of deviations.

Objectively, the cause of all these disorders resides in the conditions of our industrial life which have led to the commercialization of sex. But there are also psychological causes, such as the misconceptions which account for the unconditional acceptance of these conditions by the vast majority. Probably the most decisive misconception is a misunderstanding of the fundamental differences in the primal situation of man and woman. Obviously the identifying characteristics of the male and female roles have not been the same in all cultures and eras, yet similar basic forms are the rule everywhere, except for a few extreme divergences in remote areas. No matter how far back we go in history, even to the mythical archetypes, we encounter everywhere a given basic structure in the differentiation between the sexes. The fact is that the male and female

* An illuminating example of this was the police raid (February 12, 1968) on a party attended by the Rolling Stones at which only one girl was present—naked and in a trance-like state.

sexual organs are related in an unmistakable way and that this relatedness is carried out in the bodily structure as a whole. It is clearly to be defined as *complementary*, physiologically and otherwise, expressed in the behavior of the sexes toward one another. In its masculine and feminine interpretations, however, this complementarity can be repressed in the consciousness to permit one sex to predominate over the other.

There is one great turning point in human history when such a repression becomes quite clear: it occurred during the transition from an originally matriarchal form of civilization to a patriarchal one, which coincides with the historical leap from primary tribal cultures to the formation of nations and high civilizations. The essentially complementary sexual relationship has been blurred ever since by man's metaphysically exaggerated, almost limitless claim to domination over woman. In personal encounters between men and women, however, and in the partnership principle of marriage, that is to say, in love and in the father-mother family relationship, the original complementarity has always retained some of its validity. Here the unmistakable contradistinction of male and female characteristics is beyond dispute. These are not merely culturally established norms of role playing; behind them lie the elemental facts of procreation and conception, together with their consequences; behind them lie fatherhood and motherhood as elemental roles, noninterchangeable and complementary.

But in our sophisticated democratic industrial culture a shift has occurred, not, as is often assumed, toward the predominance of woman, in the sense of a new matriarchy, but toward a symmetry in the relation between the sexes. True symmetry is obviously impossible between man and woman for organic reasons alone. What does seem possible is a persistent approximation, an abandonment of antithetical role characteristics and of the strong differentiation between male and female modes of behavior. We see plenty of examples of this in daily life: short-haired women in trousers who hold regular jobs and are active in sports, and men carrying shopping bags and pushing baby carriages. In the United States it is even becoming common for a man to be admitted to the hospital along with his wife in order to "share" in the birth of their child.

But these, of course, are externals of little significance. The important thing in the pseudo-symmetricalization of the sexes is something else: the psychological attitude of both sexes toward the nature of their complementarity. It makes a tremendous difference whether men and women see themselves as fundamentally distinct but mutually related parts of a whole or regard themselves and their behavior toward one another as interchangeable functions in the common pursuit of sexual pleasure. The latter type of relationship, which is not concerned with life as a whole but merely with an exchange of actions, might be called *reciprocal*. When sex is seen in this light, love, mutual understanding, responsibility, and trust become objects of barter, as sexual pleasure can become an object of barter through the exchange of caresses. In this process the deeper subject-to-subject relationship is diluted; each partner becomes the other's object.

The process strikingly parallels the general commercialization of sex that we have already described and is indeed closely connected with it. Exaggerated sex propaganda and the resultant divorce of the libido from the emotional and biological life contexts help to create a psychic climate in which such a reciprocal relationship between the sexes becomes possible.

A more important factor, however, in the transformation of the complementary relation between the sexes into a reciprocal one is contemporary man's knowledge of biological processes and his consequent freedom to transcend them. His major achievement in this line is the perfecting of contraception, so that the sexual union of two people can become a matter of private barter. Thus sex loses its profoundly mysterious dual character of procreation and conception, which lies at the heart of the complementary relationship between the sexes.

A second, but no less significant factor is the anxiety about the so-called population explosion projected into sex from the social sphere. No half-way rational man can remain unmoved by the mass media's constantly reiterated warnings about overpopulation. That the warnings are justified is unquestionable; in fact, this is the first truly worldwide problem in the history of mankind. While it took man eight hundred thousand years to reach the present world population of three billion, it will take only forty years to double it to six billion. Yet birth control, unmistakably one of the most pressing social challenges of our time, involves a demand on sexual behavior that affects its biological foundation. And it is remarkable that in the worldwide debate over the pill, the question whether its use may disturb erotic relations between man and woman has hardly been raised.

Here I am not concerned with the question whether it is immoral or sinful to divorce the sexual act from the purpose of reproduction, but with the question whether to do so changes the fundamental relationship between man and woman. When the woman interferes with the ovarian cycle by taking the pill, man deposits his semen in a vacuum, so to speak. How does this affect him psychologically? May it not change his attitude toward the woman? While there can be no empirically based, experimentally confirmed answer to this question, there is no doubt that he is thus relieved of responsibility for possible procreation, a responsibility of which in normal circumstances he can never be unmindful, however great his excitement. This factor deserves the utmost attention, because the very ability to procreate by his own free decision is one of the strongest characteristics of masculinity and has been regarded as such throughout history. In this new situation, however, the procreative potential is completely subordinated to the potential for experiencing pleasure and arousing it in the female partner.

There is an essential difference between the deliberate prevention of conception (as, for instance, through *coitus interruptus*) and total preclusion of conception, in which the libido is entirely divorced from the biological function. To dream of always being able to copulate without having to worry about possible consequences is one thing; the reality is something else again. When the possibility of conception is excluded, and woman becomes solely an object of pleasure, there is a loss of the deepest, most inward and mysterious dimension of the erotic relationship; it becomes shallower, more casual, less binding, and less significant, quite possibly even less pleasurable.

We cannot evaluate this change without considering how it affects the woman and how the change in her attitude in turn affects the man. Because of the complete divorce of sexual pleasure from conception and motherhood, woman can now experience her own sexuality objectively. She can give full rein to her sexual drive and in doing so go to the utmost limit in exploiting the man's virility. Here we must bear in mind what has often been referred to as *woman's greater vitality*. Woman's weakness is, to be sure, proverbial —not merely because of the effects of her menstrual cycle but also because she is usually inferior in physical size and strength. Man's muscular strength is some 40 per cent greater than woman's; moreover, it can be significantly increased— sometimes doubled—by proper training. The capacity of the male's vital organs is much greater; the performance of a man's heart is almost double that of a woman's. But this remarkable male superiority does not apply to all bodily functions. The female is tougher biologically; she lives longer and withstands certain hardships and diseases better than the male. The life expectancy of the American woman today is six years longer than that of the American man (seventy-three years as against sixty-seven). The figures for European countries may be slightly lower, but there too women outlive men. It has not always been so; to take an extreme comparison, the analysis of prehistoric remains indicates that in the early days of the human race the life span of the average man was six years longer than that of the average woman.

The reversal is due to the conditions of modern civilization, which have considerably eased and in some respects eliminated woman's heavy biological burden of pregnancy and childbearing. As a result her biological and sexual capacity has been tremendously strengthened. By nature and because of the way they function, the female sex organs can withstand far more strenuous demands than the male organs, as the differences in structure make evident. The "tool-like" character of the male sex organ is unmistakable. Male sexuality is by nature directed toward the exclusive goal of discharge, whereas the female sex organs indicate by their structure that for woman the sexual act is only the beginning of a total process which leads far beyond the act itself. As Margaret Mead says: "The male sex act is immediately self-resolving and self-satisfying, but the female analogue is not the single copulatory experience, however self-resolving that may appear to be, but the whole cycle of pregnancy, birth and lactation."[17] This fundamental difference means that a man can father thousands of children in a lifetime (although this rarely happens in practice), while a woman is capable of conceiving and bearing some thirty at the most. On the other hand, because of the biological receptivity and passivity of her sex organs, woman is capable of meeting much more sustained sexual demands and can engage in a greater number of consecutive acts of intercourse than the male.

While the male's sexual drive is more intense than the female's because of the urge for ejaculation, it cannot be sustained so long. This shows that reciprocal sexual behavior has definite limitations.

Another consideration is the fact that the capacity for orgasm differs fundamentally in the male and the female. Here again no such thing as a reciprocal relationship exists in nature. Thus any attempt to transform the complementary sexual relationship into a reciprocal one encounters serious difficulties precisely at the crucial point: in the sexual act itself. Male and female orgasms are not "exchangeable," because they are not identical either physiologically or psychologically. While orgasm in the male is naturally linked with ejaculation, in woman it is quite different; woman's orgasm has no biological function but is an acquired response strongly dependent upon her psychic attitude. Here we may speak of a natural female sexual handicap. A woman must "learn" to have an orgasm, whereas man must learn that the woman's orgasm can heighten his own sexual experience.

As a result, the use of the pill in a reciprocal sexual relationship may lead to the woman's gaining the upper hand sexually. In natural biological circumstances woman needs man's protection, but the new situation can place man in a position where he is the one who needs protection. She can now devote to intercourse sexual energies which formerly had to sustain the whole cycle of conception, pregnancy, childbirth, and nursing. In this new relationship, in which the natural "closed seasons" for the male are drastically limited or completely eliminated, and which is intensified by the challenge of unrestrained sex propaganda, woman is able to take a more provocative stance than ever before toward the male. Now the danger arises that she may overtax both him and herself.

The woman who believes that she owes it to herself to have an orgasm in every act of intercourse is under the pressure of a self-imposed challenge. When the right to orgasm becomes a normally accepted convention, Kardiner says, it sets a socially unchallengeable standard which naturally engenders anxiety about not being able to meet it. Fear and anxiety concerning potency are becoming the contemporary social fears. The "liberating" elimination of prudish conventions in favor of sexual frankness merely creates the antithetical social convention of what Kardiner calls "orgasm compulsion." When this all too often results in failure to reach the desired goal, the woman may come to believe herself frigid, and through a reflex action of her sexual sensitivity her capacity for orgasm may be diminished. A man who achieves his own orgasm in ejaculation without bringing the woman to a climax suffers a similar psychic hurt; he is in a way reduced to impotence. The premarital petting which has a social rather than a sexual purpose can also exert a negative influence; as Margaret Mead says, "the wife feels inadequate if . . . she is not swept away—after years of learning not to be swept away."[18] Schelsky comments that the consequences of orgasm compulsion are unusually high rates of feminine frigidity and masculine impotence. Even if he does not actually become impotent, the man may lose all desire for sexual intercourse, so that the erotic relationship collapses. The man tries to escape from a demand which he finds unreasonable: having to achieve something to which the woman can force herself only with great difficulty but which she can relatively easily prevent and withhold. For the achievement of orgasm in woman depends to a great extent on a freedom from inhibition which is not guaranteed by an enlightened knowledge of sex and its mechanical processes. The elimination of inhibitions may in itself produce new ones which act as a block. A woman who strives deliberately for orgasm is wrestling with her own shadow.

This is not to say that men should withhold from women what has been called "the most intense esthetic experience known to humankind," but merely that women cannot achieve this experience in so direct and straightforward a way as men. Nonetheless, it is a mistake to set up the orgasm as a right to which woman is entitled, because a woman who comes to believe that this may turn her "weakness" into power or force so reverses the fundamental relation of the sexes. "Man's most masculine part is the one most easily intimidated." Musil's words apply not only to the man's physical vulnerability but to his psychological vulnerability too. A man may be made impotent by a woman's inept sexual behavior as much as by a kick in the groin, though not necessarily instantaneously. It may come gradually from a continuous leveling of the two kinds of sexual role. Nothing threatens the stability of a permanent erotic relationship more than for the woman to deprive the man of his active male role—something that in any case she

can never do successfully. This form of feminine emancipation rests on a fallacy and leads in a false direction. Orgasm
compulsion certainly seems to be the logical consequence,
the very apex, of feminine emancipation; but it also plainly
reveals a natural limit to woman's struggle for emancipation.

Not that emancipation itself is to be regarded as a
false direction, as many writers have alleged. Woman's liberation from social and economic dependence on man, her
attainment of equal civil rights and greater opportunities for
education, are to be wholeheartedly welcomed. But the ideal
of a total sexual equality that overlooks the fundamental
differences between the sexes is found to lead to serious
difficulties. As Herbert von Borch puts it, "woman must pay
the price of neurosis for relinquishing the power in her
weakness." Overtaxed herself by the demands of the male
world, she in turn overtaxes the man when she demands that
his first concern should be regularly to give her complete
sexual satisfaction. This is the starting point of the battle of
the sexes in our times, the permanent "war" between man
and woman that many writers have described. And there can
be no satisfactory end to this war; there can be no appease-
ment, but only steady escalation until the relationship finally
collapses. All the technical erotic expertise in which so many
magazines and manuals instruct both men and women is of
no avail. Erotic relationships onto which have been grafted
what Arnold Gehlen calls "dispossessed social instincts" and
other libidinal desires are harmed, not helped, by general
sexual instruction of this kind. Even a sex education which
concentrates on responsibility and restraint rather than ex-

perience and casualness inevitably becomes less sure of itself under the pressure of widespread sex propaganda and the seductive false models set up by the entertainment industry.

There is now a tendency to view every erotic relationship as temporary from the outset—an attitude which affects many marriages. Although, as Schelsky has said, marriage is not "primarily a sexual institution," in the modern world it is at any rate considered a profoundly erotic one. While it derives its durability from a deepening of Eros, it is being increasingly destabilized as it is stripped partially or totally of its biosocial and cultural functions, particularly the procreation and education of children. At the same time it is seriously overtaxed by the commercially manipulated challenge that turns sex into a consumer commodity. The result is a rising divorce rate. Thus the over-all picture shows a trend that might be called a retreat from Eros: man embarks on an endless pursuit of sexual stimuli which may lead him into perversion or into a withdrawal from erotic life altogether.

The chief victim of this trend is woman. Emancipation may have given her a great deal of personal independence and social security, but in a new way she is more helpless and unprotected than women of earlier ages. Our world includes a tremendous number of lonely elderly women, probably more than ever before. Except for the few who manage to create a function for themselves, these solitary women are excluded from society. Here again the matriarchal theory shows itself to be false, since society regards these old women purely as a burden. Often they are mothers who have raised their children to adulthood only to find themselves now cut off from their families and isolated from their grandchildren (Riesman speaks of the "elimination of the grandmother"). Often, too, they are the wives of successful men who have left them for younger women.

Thus contemporary woman's social security is an abstraction; it is a matter of her right to a pension and a bank account, not a matter of personal relationships in her daily life. Youth being trumps in a world that evaluates women primarily as sexual toys, the rejection and exclusion of older women is inevitable. The mature woman is forced into an ultimately losing struggle against the male world's ideal of the nubile girl, a struggle fought out in beauty shops, fashion houses, "health" clubs, and on the plastic surgeon's operating table, at a literally astronomical cost. (I refer to the reply given by defenders of the space program, when it was attacked for draining too much money away from pressing social necessities, that it cost only a fraction of what is spent annually on cosmetics.) All this is done in the name of competition for men—and in most cases, it is done in vain.

The current sex revolution is not a genuine, spontaneous revolution but a manipulated one. It is not sex that is clamoring for liberation, as claimed by the sex prophets, who themselves do not realize how much they are being influenced and manipulated by the conditions of industrial society. What the sexual psychologists, philosophers, and social reformers seeking to expand the range of human freedom and vitality—to liberate the individual from outdated social strictures, inhibitions, and restraints—have achieved may be more than they bargained for. Nor is there much promise of the more sophisticated eroticism recommended by many sexual philosophers. In its obsession with sex, contemporary society resembles those captive monkeys and cattle egrets whose sexual behavior becomes abnormal as a result of their being confined to comfortable cages. Since they have no need to hunt, fish, collect fruits and seeds, or defend their territories, and since they are more or less relieved of the responsibility of bringing up their young, they discharge their excess activism sexually and fall into perverse practices such as the rape of immature females—something that never happens in the wild. Similar changes, though in more differentiated and complicated forms, seem to take place in man's behavior within the tender trap of our industrial civilization.

It is questionable whether human nature will find this tolerable in the long run. Apes and herons may adapt themselves to captivity ad infinitum, but man will surely try to break out. Human drives, even though they may not be firmly rooted in the instincts, will not allow themselves to be betrayed indefinitely. The crisis of activism discernible behind the crisis of Eros cannot be resolved indefinitely by means of a manipulated sex boom, which threatens in many ways to turn into a sex bust. Yet in this situation it is no use preaching morality. It is not much good advocating a return to the old conventions, nor would we wish to surrender the gains that have been made. What seems imperative is to call attention to the false reciprocity in male-female sexual behavior which results from commercialization. It is time to convince society that to make sex a kind of merchandise is to jeopardize the complementary sexual behavior which nature dictates and to destroy the erotic personal relations such behavior fosters. Ultimately, however, this is a problem which cannot be solved in the sphere of Eros alone; its causes lie elsewhere.

3
THE CRISIS
OF ACTIVISM AND
AGGRESSION

Today aggression is the most acute of all international problems that concern the coexistence of nations and national communities and the coexistence of individuals and groups. Yet it is not possible to define aggressiveness with precision in psychological terms; being involved in many forms of human behavior, it is not always clearly identifiable. One characteristic alone is plain: its most obvious social expression everywhere and always is found in warfare and soldiering. The problem of aggressiveness is thus essentially a male problem. With very few exceptions society has never cast women in a militarily aggressive role corresponding to the role of the male warrior. The Amazon armies of classical antiquity are a legend—perhaps a sadistic male fantasy. The female bodyguards of the kings of Dahomey, whose ferocious cruelty is frequently cited, is a case by itself; modern diagnostic methods would probably assign

111

most of these guards to an "intersex."* For the male, on the other hand, the cultural and social stylization of the warrior type has been decisive throughout the ages. Specialized though this type may be, it still codetermines the traditional male role. Even as a revolutionary and an antimilitarist, man models himself on the warrior and the fighter, as can be seen from bourgeois and working-class rebellions and from the peasant armies of the sixteenth century. Hence nothing affects the male more acutely than the general disrepute into which militant behavior has fallen in the world of liberal democracy. The inevitable transformation of the male role into a harmless, passive one is a trend which negates the traditional male image dominant throughout the centuries—and which probably negates man's own nature too.

Let us look first at the typical behavior of the fighting man. All forms of soldiering have fostered a warlike attitude bent on conquering or annihilating enemies: the soldier is a male specialist authorized by society to use force and to kill. Thus his training must make a virtue of hostility and aggression, and he must be always ready to die for the sake of his objective, the conquest of the enemy. This basic pattern of fighting behavior is found in all forms of civilization, although it may become more complex in response to certain moral and metaphysical influences, as is demonstrated by the

---

* "Intersex" individuals are not hermaphrodites, but their chromosome structure is abnormal. Women of this type have extra male chromosomes, and this increases their physical capacities. Modern tests for women athletes are based on this anomaly.

different fighting styles of medieval knights, Indians of the American prairies, and Japanese samurai.

Since the beginning of European civilization in Greece, the hero image has been decisive in determining the fighting behavior of Western man. Originally, says Karl Reinhardt, the hero is "preeminently the epic hero—in the Western tradition the Homeric one, and his cousin, the hero of the tragedies, the Nordic, stylized hero later modified by ethical, social, or cultural requirements into the hero of the epics of chivalry, the baroque or classicistic hero."[1]

The child's simple visualization of the hero as a man who dedicates his life to a higher purpose for the common good in a warlike task that may be beyond his strength can be applied to all these concepts of the European hero. The greater the task, the greater the hero; and only the really great heroes can perform the really great tasks. Yet while the hero transcends the common measure, he does not transcend the measure of man as such. Although the concept of heroism is of mythic origin and partakes of this mythologization in real life, its ultimate standards are those of its earthly exemplars, and it exists within the bounds of normal life. "The true hero must be accessible; he must not be exempt from criticism. The hero . . . is part of the treasury of man's archetypal self-images, both as he would like to be and as he knows himself to be. In the hero man celebrates his own triumphs, desires, perils, victories, defeats, fears, courage, self-conquests, sacrifices, griefs, and so on."[2] The hero must not triumph by magic or by virtue of any special advantages.

He may be in league with divine powers, but never to the point of being invulnerable. He must be capable of suffering and of making mistakes; he must not be immune to the risks of death and defeat or even of dishonor and humiliation. He must overcome his enemy in direct personal confrontation and must himself be open to confrontation and defeat by the enemy. While, like Ulysses, he may rely on guile and cunning as well as strength, his adversary must be his equal in rank. Only then is the battle chivalrous and fair. Only victory over an equally strong or a stronger adversary can confer heroic stature.

The direction which the military profession and its technologies have now taken runs counter to this heroic concept of soldiering. While the latter was always an ideal, only to be approximated in real life, it has become utterly utopian in the climate of today. The old-style hero has been forced out of modern warfare, which has no use for chivalry. The concept of heroism has been totally reversed: it is no longer the deeds of individual fighters that determine the outcome of wars, but the supply and successful deployment of men and matériel. This shift was signalized after World War I by the erection of a monument to the Unknown Soldier, a "hero" who was everyone, and no one. Heroism became even more anonymous and universal in World War II, when "total mobilization" and "total war" eventually led to the conscription of children, women, and old men into war service, both active and passive. The grandmother knitting in the bomb shelter amid the thunder of explosions, the child serving as a civil defense messenger or auxiliary fire fighter, both heroes, helped make an end of the traditional chivalric concept of the hero.

For the unknown soldiers and civilians of our major wars are, after all, only passive victims of our monstrous war machines, to which all are harnessed alike. However great their personal achievements may be—even if they distinguish themselves by extraordinary feats such as those of the fighter pilots who shot down over a hundred enemy aircraft—they still remain part of the machine. Their individual deeds are swamped in its overall impact. In modern war the crucial decisions are made elsewhere: in supply and logistics, in the armament factories, in scientific laboratories. They often involve the killing, starving, or annihilation of unarmed civilians. There is nothing heroic about this kind of thing, which explains why no genuine heroic epic has been written to celebrate any fighter in the last two world wars.

The fact that modern literature has produced no truly heroic figure to rank with the great historical models is not owing to the much-discussed antiheroic bias of the contemporary writer. Serious attempts have in fact been made to create convincing contemporary heroic figures, but with little success, while a whole series of strikingly effective works have debunked or unmasked the would-be hero. The characteristic Hemingway hero, for example, is a brave man who turns out in the end to have been a dupe or a victim. To be a brave, manly loser, like the protagonist of *The Old Man and the Sea*, is as far as heroism can go in Hemingway.

World War II produced one man who by a nonroutine action ended a conflict between two nations which had engulfed the whole world: the flyer who, by pressing a button, dropped the atom bomb on Hiroshima. While he certainly meets the requirement that the hero overcome the enemy and force a decision by a momentous action, it is obvious that the bombing of Hiroshima was not a heroic deed. It is typical that this man was not celebrated as a great hero but remained anonymous for a long time and after some sensational publicity sank back again into anonymity. It is typical, too, that the public is not even sure of his identity, because the flyer who claimed to have dropped the bomb and to have suffered a nervous breakdown as a result was accused by military authorities of lying. This case demonstrates particularly clearly the marginal position of military heroism in our time. In this man the "hero" has become an anonymous functionary, the lackey of mass destruction. By contrast we can still think of von Richthofen, the most famous pilot of World War I, as a hero, not only because he had the highest score of enemy planes shot down but because he chivalrously spared planes that had run out of ammunition and let them get away. By World War II such chivalrous behavior could no longer be officially condoned.

As war machines and armaments are perfected and their performances improved, chivalry can no longer be the prerogative of the individual, because "the business of war" becomes a kind of industrialized teamwork. Whether to use or refrain from using a particular weapon is not for the individual to decide. Instead of being a contest between two human opponents taking equal risks, war is a confrontation between widely deployed engines of mass destruction. The development of weapons is a particularly striking aspect of this transformation. In little over a century we have progressed from the Colt (1883), the first fully perfected firearm and still to many boys a symbol of chivalrous fighting, to nuclear weapons. It took the technological revolution more than a half century to proceed from the Colt to the machine gun; fifty years later came the atom bomb. The course of this development leads from the rapid, accurate firing of a hand weapon at an opponent who is presumably on his guard—the myth of the West as it is still presented daily to millions of people on film and television—to a capacity for killing millions of people in one strike.

We must bear in mind what this means for the potential conduct of wars and for aggressive warlike behavior, considering that we already have bombs millions of times more powerful than the first one. Individual weapons exist whose explosive force surpasses the destructive energy released in all the wars waged by mankind up to the present day. This explosive energy is concentrated in a single weapon, which can be delivered by one aircraft or rocket to any spot on earth. Many such bombs exist, and new ones are constantly being manufactured. Five countries have them already: the United States, Russia, Great Britain, France, and China. It would even be possible today to keep bombs of this type constantly in orbit around the earth in satellites, ready for use at any time. There is no defense against them.

The possession of such power, on such a scale, is something unprecedented in history. With the discovery of atomic energy man has reached the absolute terminus in the development of means of destruction. He now has within his grasp, in the truest sense of the word, the colossal energy of the sun, so that he is capable of producing on earth artificial solar catastrophes which surpass all the terrors of the ancient myths. Science has shown the absurdity of man's primeval, mythical fear of eclipses, or fear that the sun may suddenly fall from the heavens or draw closer and burn everything up. But the mythic fear is now transposed to man himself as a fear of his own actions. The existing stockpile of thermonuclear bombs is sufficient to reduce the whole earth to a moon landscape. If these bombs are used on an unrestricted scale, not only is all mankind, friend or foe, destined to perish, but also all animals and plants and the very air we breathe. Given the range and speed of modern jet planes and rockets, this can happen in a few hours. Man's power over earthly creation has become so great that he can bring it to an end, an end such as was prophesied for the gods in *Edda:*

> *The sun turns pale*
> *From the searing flashes*
> *Of the flaming sword*
> *Which he wields in his right hand.*
> *Rocks crumble to dust,*
> *Giantesses topple,*
> *The sky bursts asunder,*
> *Heroes go down to the dark halls*
> *Where Hela dwells.*

This tremendous destructive power which man now controls, power over the mightiest cosmic force, solar energy itself, makes the traditional image of the hero obsolete forever. Long foreshadowed in the progressive evolution of military technology and organization, his eclipse has now become plain for all to see. Thus the trend which began in the nineteenth century with the invention of mechanical weapons and high explosives has reached its logical conclusion. Under the impact of the machine gun and rapid-fire artillery, modes of professional fighting began to change. Possibly the most decisive change that over-all technological progress has produced, though not the most obvious one, is the *total withdrawal of the commanders and generals from the zone of fire.* The more inexorably the enlisted man has been exposed to weapons of mass destruction—to the point where even genuinely brave men ready to die for their ideals can speak of themselves as "cannon fodder"—the farther the staff officers have withdrawn from a real scene of combat. It is not a question of courage or the lack of it. They must be in a safe position in order to direct operations; they cannot risk leaving their armies "headless." Nevertheless, their physical safety is better protected than that of anybody else, not only in their armies but even including the civilian population. They are ceasing to "look death in the eye" themselves, but merely look on at the death of others. The original situation where the general led—or at any rate accompanied—his troops into battle has been reversed: the position of a commanding officer has become a kind of life insurance. At Stalingrad, at Dien Bien Phu, in the German *Afrika Korps,* generals set themselves apart; generals become important prisoners; generals survive.

To question the moral qualities of military leaders would be beside the point, which is that modern technological warfare, relying on extraordinary destructive weapons and a perfected communications system, must lead to this *total separation of fighting troops and high command.* Everybody senses that today's great "war heroes," the celebrated ones to whom the highest decorations are awarded, are in fact nothing but uniformed battlefield managers who direct events from their desks. This applies even to com-manders of mobile troops, such as the legendary Field Marshals Rommel and Montgomery who, according to their own notebooks and memoirs, kept out of range of the shooting. The withdrawal of the commander from actual combat has become complete as a result of nuclear weapons and strategy: though military bases, industrial centers, and cities may be reduced to ashes, the generals will be sitting in fallout-proof super-shelters.

The present military situation is such that if the two great atomic powers, the United States and the Soviet Union, mobilized their total potential they could destroy one another in a few hours—and the rest of the world into the bargain. What has so far restrained them is not entirely clear. Possibly their mutual hostility is not as intense as the cold war made it seem. No doubt the responsible leaders of both these great nations have genuine scruples, despite all their show of being ready to go to all lengths. No doubt they are afraid for their people—perhaps even afraid *of* them.

Each is afraid that even if his own country won, it would be devastated beyond recovery. Thus the original purpose of every war—to safeguard and promote society's existence and continued development—is wholly perverted. For this reason most experts believe that a fairly even balance of strength (causing the attacker to fear that he will be annihilated too) has a stabilizing effect, the so-called atomic stalemate.

Since the early 1950's military theorists have been racking their brains to find a way of stabilizing this highly jeopardized "equilibrium of fear." If one of two opposing powers became convinced, on the basis of erroneous information, that the other was about to attack, the first power might feel driven to anticipate such a strike at any cost. Another danger is that neither power knows exactly what defenses the other may have against the type of attack which it has devised. If one side begins to develop a new defensive system that could considerably diminish or neutralize the impact of the offensive weapons of the other, the latter might feel compelled to strike first. The same applies to the development of a new system of attack. Thus the atomic stalemate provides no real guarantee of lasting peace and no guarantee that atomic energy will not be used for military ends. War seems to have become unthinkable but not impossible.

This realization has produced a new school of military strategists who decided to "think about the unthinkable," to make a thorough study of the conduct of war in the atomic era and to assess the chances of surviving. One of the school's leading spokesmen is the American physicist Herman Kahn, who published a book on thermonuclear war in 1960 and another book in 1966 entitled *On Escalation*.[3] Kahn, who has built up a private research institute with a staff of seventy-five, holds no official position, but it can be assumed that he exercises considerable influence on American military policy. By working out the possibilities of a future atomic war as an intellectual game using computerized models, he concluded that even a nuclear war would not necessarily mean total annihilation, but could be kept within what he terms tolerable limits. He does not agree that all-out nuclear war would mean the end of the human race. Assessing the atomic potential of the two great nuclear powers, he estimated that at the very worst, one-tenth of the present American population would survive, that this could be increased to two-thirds by providing some protection against radiation, and that large-scale protection by all available means would raise the proportion to over three-quarters. Kahn also developed a theory which turned the currently accepted view of all-out nuclear war upside down. Future wars, he says, will not necessarily begin, as most people fear, with the surprise deployment of a nation's total nuclear potential. Even in the atomic era this type of attack still remains the last, extreme resort of warfare.

Kahn's *escalation theory* distinguishes forty-four rungs and five decisive thresholds on the ladder between cold war and "spasm or insensate war." Only on the third threshold lying between rung 20 and rung 21 does the transition occur from conventional warfare with threats of atomic strikes to the first local nuclear attack. Then come the rungs of semi-total atomic war: target bombing of military objectives, industries, and large cities, and lastly, all-out war, leading to Armageddon. Kahn believes that escalation can be halted right up to rung 43. While the conduct of wars since World War II—for instance, those in Korea and Vietnam—seems to indicate that he may be right, his theory cannot be guaranteed. Above all there is no guarantee that, in an emergency, escalation would not proceed too rapidly to be halted. Kahn himself has had the foresight to make his family home far enough away from New York City to be beyond the fallout zone.

Kahn's reply to the question whether the world could survive a thermonuclear war was: "That depends on how the war is to be fought. In the worst war we have analyzed theoretically, more than a hundred million Americans, a hundred million Russians, two to three hundred million Europeans, and almost the whole Chinese population were killed. This is a war in which the governments don't care what happens to their own people and are interested solely in killing off the enemy population. But I can't imagine any government acting in that way." In answer to the question whether anyone would be able to live in such a world, he replied: "History offers no example of the survivors envying the dead."

Such an answer seems to confirm the suspicion that a thinker of Kahn's type represents a terrible danger to the world. Atomic strategists of his kind advocate preventive nuclear war behind a front of scientific ethical "neutrality."

These military technocrats show plainly enough how completely separate the administration of wars has become from the actual fighting of them. Such "civilian militarists" are the counterparts of bureaucratic manager-generals who live in a world of abstractions with a fixed enemy orientation. Their idea of living with the bomb (and using it) seems to depend upon their being included among the leaders who will form the only social group with a real chance of survival.

In the East, too, there are strategists who take essentially the same stance, as shown by Marshal V. D. Sokolovsky's book *Military Strategy*, published in 1962.[4] This book, written by a team of experts, is even more indicative of the thinking of today's top military leaders inasmuch as these authors are professionals, not civilian theorists like Kahn and his cohorts. Sokolovsky is a former chief of staff of the Soviet Army and first deputy defense minister of the U.S.S.R. He and his comrades support the escalation theory in an even more radical form than Kahn: far from regarding the use of nuclear weapons as a last resource of military strategy, they take it for granted. They believe that a modern major war between world powers will automatically be fought under the law of atomic terror. They acknowledge from the outset that strategy has been changed fundamentally by the exigencies of atomic weapons and that conventional methods of attack and defense have lost all significance. A war of the future will be decided not by a series of battles but by annihilating strikes at enemy centers. All that is left for conventional forces to do is occupy enemy territory and mop up pockets of resistance.

The Russians also say frankly that they do not believe the atomic stalemate can prevent nuclear war, which they regard as inevitable. In their atomic strategy, therefore, great importance is attached to building up morale, that is, strengthening the resistance of their own social order so that it will be able to withstand nuclear attacks without collapsing. Even though one probable objective of this strategy is to deter the West, it does demonstrate the military leadership's uncompromising determination to reconcile itself to the terrors of an atomic war.

The views of these military authorities and their advisers show beyond doubt that in the present situation war has finally become a crime. Wars are now planned scientifically, with cold logic and the most up-to-date mathematical techniques—a procedure which is not only incapable of preventing war but may even prepare the way for it. On these grounds the American mathematician James R. Newman is sharply critical of Kahn's work, which, he says, is a moral treatise on mass murder: how to plan it, how to commit it, how to get away with it, and how to justify it. And Oskar Morgenstern, who in collaboration with the mathematician John von Neumann invented the theory of games, writes, in his book *The Question of National Defense:* "War is, of course, not less absurd at this time than it ever will be in the future; but that does not mean that this absurdity is everywhere recognized and therefore becomes less effective."[5]

Morgenstern, who has also been an adviser to the American government for many years, supports the theory of a thermonuclear stalemate. Since he believes that the stalemate is seriously endangered, and since, as he says, "moral or religious considerations have failed to stop wars," he seeks a technological solution to the problem. "War has to become technologically impossible in order to be stopped."[6] Convinced that nothing can halt technological progress, and hence that the international arms race cannot be stopped, he draws the conclusion that technological progress must be internationally democratized. Consequently he supports the demand of the great nuclear physicist Niels Bohr for an "open world." Only in a world in which men and ideas can freely cross national frontiers can we be sure that major scientific or technological innovations will not be kept secret. Only in such a world can we be sure that no nation can make the dangerous discovery of a secret weapon.

Morgenstern goes even further: he thinks we should deliberately help the enemy to arm. To prevent his being tempted to strike first by an imaginary or real weakness, we should make him so strong that he feels invulnerable. "In view of modern technology, of speedy weapons delivery from any point on earth to any other, it is in the interest of the United States for Russia to have an invulnerable retaliatory force and vice versa."[7] According to Morgenstern, the atomic stalemate can be stabilized only by maintaining an arms balance, because only this will permit limited "dueling wars" which will not be escalated into total atomic war intended to annihilate the enemy. He believes that this goal can be attained. In present circumstances he believes the prospect of limited war between atomic powers to be an illusion: "As it is, the probability of a large thermonuclear war occurring appears to be significantly larger than the probability of its not occurring."[8]

In view of the constant threat of atomic war, we may well ask whether there is now any sense in maintaining a conventional military system. In the face of potential atomic strategy all the operative and tactical functions of conventional forces seem practically meaningless. And yet the recruiting, training, and arming of conventional troops goes on as if nothing had happened. Military experts have indeed complained that training systems and the concept of combat discipline are still based on eighteenth-century ideas. This, however, is only partly true. According to modern military sociologists, traditional troop units are now engaged in internal regrouping. The American military sociologist Morris Janowitz, for instance, points to a radical change in the concept of military authority. He believes that the traditional authoritarian control has lost much of its validity and is being replaced by manipulation, persuasion, and group consensus. The military, he thinks, is being democratized and civilized.

The slogan "citizens in uniform" coined in Germany by Count Wolf von Baudissin points in the same direction. Baudissin is one of the fathers of the "inner guidance" concept, which seeks to reform the structure of authority. Of course this concept is still far from being realized; moreover, it is under strong attack from military leaders. Hans-Georg von Studnitz contradicts Baudissin and says there is no such thing as a "citizen in uniform."[9] In support of this he quotes Baudissin's own words: "The 'citizen in uniform' is by definition a soldier who knows what he is for and what he is against. It would be ideal if a young man entering the army could bring this knowledge with him as a judgment which our nation's education and cultural institutions had helped him to reach. But whether this goal can ever be achieved in our society seems to me more than doubtful." Upholding the traditional concept of authority, Studnitz attacks the "primacy of the administration," that is, amateurs in official positions and their control over military experts.

The struggle to reorganize the military services in conformity with an open democratic society seems ultimately to be inhibited by a faint feeling of absurdity— although not many representatives of the services will admit this. Soldiering today is carried on under the abiding shadow of the atomic threat. But it is not this alone which changes it so radically and which characterizes contemporary forms of military organization. Hand in hand with the technological evolution of armies goes a bureaucratic evolution. All military organizations today are heavily burdened with indispensable bureaucratic machinery. Max Weber was aware that in modern nations the real control is exercised by civilian as well as military authorities. Even the high-ranking officer, he said, today directs his battles from an office. "The modern mass army, too, is a bureaucratic army, and the officer is a special type of official, distinct from the knight, the *condottiere*, the chieftain, or the Homeric hero."[10]

Morris Janowitz says that in order to analyze the current military services as a social system, we must start with the assumption that for a long time they have been showing more and more of the characteristics of all great nonmilitary bureaucracies. The differences are diminishing as the result of continuous technological changes leading to enormous expansion of the armed services, to their extreme dependence on the rest of society, and to alterations in their own social structure.[11] Military leadership is steadily becoming a specialized professional field which includes a great many bureaucratic functions. Janowitz cites figures for the growth of military bureaucracy in the United States: at the time of the Civil War in 1861, it amounted to 0.7 per cent; by 1954 it had risen to 17.5 per cent. In the Civil War 93.2 per cent of Army personnel were engaged in purely military functions; by 1954 the percentage assigned to actual fighting had dropped to 28.8 per cent." In the Navy and Air Force that percentage is even lower. The military services of all industrialized nations show a similar trend.

This bureaucratization leads to a reduction of personal responsibility among lower- and medium-ranking commissioned officers which conflicts with the alleged democratization through cooperation and teamwork. In an article on what is wrong with the German Army, Helmut Schmidt notes the tendency of high-ranking officers to cover themselves by formulating their orders so meticulously that they leave no leeway for those who have to execute them, thus discouraging initiative among their subordinates.[12] This state of affairs probably prevails in most armies.

Certainly no real democratization of military leadership can be detected in today's armed services. As in contemporary industrial and governmental bureaucracies, there is just a show of democratization under the guise of cooperation, but not enough to conceal the fact that the base and the top of the pyramid are getting farther and farther apart. Cooperation exists only within the very exclusive leadership groups, as is the case in industry and politics. The incorporation of psychologists and sociologists into the military machine ultimately serves the old structure of authority, because they direct and manipulate group relationships. The real commanders are still the heads of the military bureaucracy and technocracy, and they are in a position to drop the nuclear sword of Damocles at any time, no matter what the conventional military organizations may or may not do.

The decisive fact about the evolution of modern military organizations and the kind of warfare they promote is that the civilian population is increasingly involved in modern war. As Janowitz says: "Indeed, the impact of technological developments during the last half-century has had the consequence of 'civilianizing' the military profession and of blurring the distinction between the civilian and the military. Weapons of mass destruction socialize danger to the point of equalizing the risks of warfare between soldier and civilian."[13] He is an optimist: today three civilians are killed in Vietnam for every soldier. Said Rudolf Augstein, editor-in-chief of *Der Spiegel:* "Napalm burns to death ten noncombatants, always including a child, before it accounts for a single Vietcong partisan. The 'bag' of enemy dead is counted every day. . . . What do the fifty-nine who died at the

Berlin wall amount to in comparison with the hundred thousand women and children burned to death in Vietnam through the white man's arrogance—and who will be followed by another hundred thousand?"[14] The military might as well be using the atomic bomb.

It may be objected that the war in Vietnam is a civil war and that the partisan warfare imposed by the enemy has its own laws. But is not every war a civil war today? And in a satellite-encircled world, open to attack from the air and crisscrossed with communications, is not every war potentially a global civil war? In addition, the technological perfection of warfare today makes the usual inhumanity of war automatic. Wars have always claimed civilian victims and been accompanied by deliberate atrocities, but technotronic war multiplies the incidental victims and atrocities ad infinitum. It also enables its commanders simultaneously to utter humanitarian phrases, provide genuine relief measures for the civilian population, and drop napalm bombs.

Perfected technotronic war demands and breeds a schizophrenic consciousness and conscience, and this finally leads to flirtation with the idea of atomic suicide as a last resort of self-defense. Herman Kahn has actually advised the Americans to use their superatomic bombs to blow the world to pieces in case of defeat, and similar ideas have been expressed elsewhere. In a public debate, Swiss and Austrian experts discussed the possibility of a small nation committing tactical suicide in order to escape occupation by a hostile superpower. Such speculations reveal an extremely high level of aggression—which is said to be one of the psychological causes of suicide. Among the warlike Mundugumors in the South Seas, for example, a man may commit suicide before his enemy's eyes in anger over the possibility of being defeated. Lawrence of Arabia describes an Arab leader who, overcome by anger at the sight of raped and massacred women and children, in a futile gesture of individual defiance threw himself into the concentrated fire of a superior enemy. To advocate tactical suicide is to appeal to this angry, frustrated aggression which turns against the self.

In an era when intellectual games are played with the "doomsday bomb," any attempt to restructure and democratize the conventional military organization serves only to heighten the discrepancy between the contemporary soldier and his old chivalrous image. Nowhere is this ironical discrepancy, this divergence from heroic ideals, more evident than among the enlisted men in combat units of modern armies. The literature of the First World War was already full of their disillusionment. The Swiss military expert Colonel Rolf R. Bigler has made a study of the "isolated" soldier who lets himself be taken prisoner instead of fighting. Bigler asserts that the majority of soldiers behave in this way and cites the findings of American military sociologists that on the average, only fifteen men out of a hundred use their weapons at all during an action.[15] He also shows that lofty ideological war aims and the philosophical, religious, and national ideals behind them mean little to the average soldier.

What does the soldier really fight for? To quote Bigler:

¶ National war aims, the fight against Fascist tyranny, star-spangled banners, and crusades for freedom— these slogans and symbols did not mean much to the soldier, although they were completely in line with his thinking. But he never looked to these symbols which give war its meaning for support. He was not fighting because he was afraid of being punished if he didn't. Even his feelings of hatred for the enemy were a minor factor. He never even saw the enemy in action: he saw objectives, helmets, movements, and strange uniforms, but no individuals whom he could have hated personally. Two organizations were making war on each other; two countries were trying to bring each other to their knees; but the logical assumption, the one that had always been posited: namely that the front-line troops on both sides must hate each other's guts—this turned out to be completely false. Great as was the shock produced by this realization, it was surpassed by the astonishment aroused by the remarkable disclosure that most soldiers were actually fighting for "their buddies" and their immediate superiors! Not, mark it, *by order of* these superiors but *for* them.[16]

Bigler is referring here to the exceptional officer who was respected by his men and whom they viewed as an ally. Most soldiers, however, are indifferent to their officers, and a considerable number even hate them.

But so far as the fighting potential of a unit is concerned, the most important factor is loyalty to the small group. Where this exists, the soldiers fight for one another, in order to protect each other and to stand the common test. Where this does not exist, where a unit consists of isolated soldiers, the fighting potential is extremely low. Military sociologists believe that the latter situation, which predominates in most armies, results from poor military training. They attribute it to the outdated structure of authority and to false indoctrination which stresses discipline and underemphasizes group loyalty. Bigler describes the isolated soldier as a passive one:

¶ Everything indicates that however well disciplined and well trained the soldier may be, he is in danger of regressing under fire to inadequate patterns of behavior—inadequate in the sense that they do not fit the situation in which he finds himself. The organization is vast and he no longer feels himself a member of it. In the terrible landscape of death he steps temporarily out of his role, relinquishing the rights and duties of the organization. This does not mean that he runs away like a coward. He is much more likely to keep on confronting danger *passively* and remain wherever he happens to be, or to trot along obediently behind the sergeant. Everything seems to him meaningless and pointless.[17]

But perhaps the reasons for behavior of this kind are to be sought in a completely different area. Perhaps they lie in the soldier's awareness, no less real for being unformulated, of the dilemma in which his whole profession is caught. Perhaps they lie in the pacification of the consciousness which results automatically from knowledge of the atomic threat and which makes the soldier himself resist his own aggressive tendencies, now activated by military service. Man's inherent proclivity for aggression, though encouraged and exploited by military organizations, is checked by his realization of the new historical situation, in which aggression and bellicose behavior are no longer admissible. Janowitz also notes that the *conditional* freedom from war which has ensued from the atomic menace may be transformed in the soldier's consciousness into a *matter of principle*, thus making him psychically and physically less inclined to fight. The longer the global armistice lasts, the more intensively these inarticulated yet logical notions develop within the soldier. Because of their explosive potential, however, they tend to be repressed from consciousness. Strategic military games and maneuvers, despite their martial appearance, are permeated by the tacit agreement of military nonaggression. Apart from their value as exercises, their significance is coming to be purely symbolic.[18]

Man's traditional role as a fighting soldier—endorsed, legalized, often glorified as an approved channel for his aggressive impulses—has undergone radical changes due to the modern hypertrophy of weapons technology. Even Russia, with its ideological indoctrination of troops that is rigorously controlled from above, has not been completely successful in preventing these inner conflicts in its soldiers. A case in point is the detachment of Russian troops under Vlassov and the "volunteer" units from the occupied countries that fought on Germany's side against Russia in the

Second World War. Even group manipulation based on the findings of social psychology cannot eliminate the artificial schizophrenia which pervades military life today, a schizophrenia that has led to an extraordinary increase of what in military terminology is called "treason." The tension between the extreme attitudes toward life which are inculcated in everybody makes it possible for many people to take a short step in one direction or another and wind up in a diametrically opposed position. The situation produces the traitor, not vice versa.

What, then, is left of heroism? What remains of a thousand years of stylized and idealized male aggression? Karl Reinhardt has drawn attention to the ambivalent attitude toward heroism shown by Nietzsche, whose *Thus Spake Zarathustra* was carried by German World War I volunteers in their packs on the battlefields of Langemarck and Ypres. Reinhardt shows that Nietzsche's critique exposes the playactor within the hero when the heroic mask is torn away. "But what this mask conceals," says Reinhardt, "is something which, like much else, has good reason to hide itself: a will to hold power and to overpower, from the most brutal manifestations to the most idealistic—this is the primordial driving force behind the lust for interference with everything foreign, everything not akin to itself."[19] Reinhardt also recalls Nietzsche's appeal in *Zarathustra:* "In the name of my love and hope I beseech you: do not cast out the hero in your soul!" He points to the heroic transformation which so clearly occurred in members of the Resistance during the Nazi terror. "Heroism, however great the pressure upon it, is something other than mute surrender and inflexible obedience. All the more, then, is the volunteer spirit the mask which power covets. The call for a positive hero, under Hitler or in Russia, is totalitarian power's bid for the prestige of the hero while using him as a slave."

In such circumstances it may indeed be more heroic to say no than to say yes. Thus while the coward goes to war, the brave man may reject war. And the man who refuses to shoot, that is, to pull the trigger, the man who simply refuses to go along or who even has the courage to take a stand, may be acting more heroically than the man who merely obeys. Many people found themselves in this situation under National Socialism; many find themselves in it today under Communism, and even within the more covertly manipulated Western democratic society.

With this, a completely new stylization of male aggressive tendencies emerges: a shift of the heroic from a public into an apparently private area. In the Resistance the individual assumed responsibility for everybody else without being delegated to do so by any public agency or official public opinion. The hero went underground as a guerrilla, a partisan. There are many indications that future wars, provided they can be kept within conventional limits, are increasingly likely to be partisan wars, and not necessarily Communist ones. Only in America is it always taken for granted that national and social liberation movements are Communist-inspired. This too often leads the United States to back the wrong side, namely the totalitarian rulers, thus virtually forcing the rebels into the arms of the Communists. We need only to think of the rebellions in East Berlin in 1953 and in Hungary in 1956 to know that resistance is not synonymous with Communism. Even the Cuban revolt was not originally Communist, nor was the one in Haiti. With regard to heroism a point of particular interest and significance is that partisan warfare makes extraordinary demands on fighting morale. Hence morality itself is used as a weapon, not only insofar as the partisans' personal lives are concerned, but also with regard to their conduct toward the civilian population. "They really seem to have rediscovered the secret of every viable morality: self-abnegation. It is clear enough that this behavior would win over any people in the world, not merely primitive peoples."[20]

Without seeking to glorify partisan warfare, we may state that as a basic tactic in every war of liberation against totalitarian oppression, it probably represents the only outlet for male aggression which conscience can justify in the world of today. In any other military form, male aggression can no longer be justified. This is why male aggressiveness has become one of the greatest problems of contemporary society, both within and without the military— all the more so because we are obliged to censure it as a criminal form of behavior and repress our consciousness of it. But since censure does not get rid of it, what happens? Aggression is a highly mutable and adaptable instinct and in the course of history has assumed even the most pacific guises, coming forth as salvation, as charity, or as a benign force for freedom. It was shortly after World War II that the United States War Department was rechristened the Department of Defense, and since then no power has ever seen itself as an aggressor. All over the world purely "defensive" forces confront one another, armed to the teeth in the interests of peace. Commenting on Apollo 11 in *The New York Times* on *Moon*day, July 21, 1969, Lewis Mumford labeled the space expedition "a symbolic act of war" claiming to be "for peace" and adds bitterly: "on the same level as the Air Force's monstrous hypocrisy—'Our Profession is Peace.' "

Does this "peace hypocrisy" have its good side— something like Freud's "cultural hypocrisy" that helps to maintain civilization "because the capacity for culture of the present generation of men may not suffice, unaided, for the task?"[21] Man's natural aptitude for peace is indeed inadequate to maintain it. But should people be taught that pacifism is morally so right and aggression so wrong that one's aggressive intentions must never be openly stated? The danger in doing so is that, rather than educate men toward true peacefulness, this will merely lead them to repress all awareness of aggressive tendencies. The aggressive strivings of individuals, groups, and nations then become invisible, vanish beneath the magic cloak of ideals and ideologies and appear transformed into their opposite. By such adaptation and subterfuge aggression escapes conscious control and becomes even more difficult—even impossible—to restrain and subdue. Nor is such unconscious aggression less dangerous than open aggression: it may indeed be far more malignant in its various disguises.

Even more destructive to male life than the crisis of aggression is the tendency inherent in the hyperorganized society of today to inhibit male activism. In the occupational world of industrial bureaucracy, the majority find themselves tied up in an administrative straightjacket, hamstrung by red tape, and bedeviled by memoranda, directives, security measures, and insurance precautions. The organized efficiency that aims at maximum productivity and maximum profits requires the worker to adapt to duties that are highly specialized, one-sided, superficial, repetitious. To function with a minimum of conflict in these conditions, a man learns to conform, to be passive and dependent—to sacrifice his initiative and the wholeness of his personality.

The villain is not the greedy individual manager, of course, but the superorganizational framework characteristic of the most advanced enterprises of our time, those powerful combines that develop by ingesting numbers of smaller units. The responsibilities and opportunities for initiative formerly distributed among a large number of individuals tend to be concentrated in a few hands within the giant corporations. This is more than a continuation of an already existing trend: it represents a qualitative leap. The technotronic society imposes its own "natural laws" upon everyone impartially, as though it were truly some monstrous new artificial force of nature.

In Hermann Schmidt's "The Development of Technology Seen as Phases of Human Evolution" three historical stages are posited. The first is termed the stage of the tool, ranging from the paleolithic stone artifact to the beginnings of the steam engine in the eighteenth century. During this stage the use of the tool was optional; man decided whether or not to employ it. As industrial capitalism developed, however, research, technology, and economics merged into a new unity with laws of its own. Schmidt's second stage is that of the machine which performs labor or produces power, and the third stage is that of automation. At the first stage, both physical energy and mental effort are contributed by the individual. At the second stage, physical energy is technologically objectified; and at the third stage, even mental effort is technologically objectified. Whereas the early tools merely reinforced or extended man's physical capacities, the machines of the intermediate period relieved him of the necessity for contributing his own physical energy to do the job. Now, under automation, the whole cycle of performance has been "emancipated" from the individual and thus objectified, "including the connecting links of conscious supervision and direction."[22]

Thus the sources of energy, labor, and planning are all under the control of a common unified law: the law of interdependence and interpenetration of parts. It controls the superstructured production combines, the megasocieties, the power blocs, the great nations. Bureaucratization represents the necessary administrative side of this inexorable process. The tendency of every bureaucracy to become a super-bureaucracy, continually invading new areas of organization, does not stem basically from the individual bureaucrats' desire for power, as satirized in Parkinson's Law. It is part of an inescapable rational process of socio-economic evolution.

Bureaucratization is particularly evident in totalitarian states, but democratic countries too have their top-level organizations through which the constituent parts can be combined, forced to cooperate, and supervised. The technological instruments that support the bureaucratic machine, from telephone and typewriter to the computer, are instruments of authoritative control. In the necessary course of their development they constantly seek to merge in an ever-tighter network of bureaucratic supermachinery. Thus it becomes increasingly evident that bureaucracy as an all-embracing process is establishing itself as a new form of authority. It is no accident that so much social criticism, in the East and the West, concerns itself explicitly or implicitly with the impotence of the individual and the power of the machine.*

Although small, tightly knit systems of human groups may continue to exist as survivors of a bygone era and to reconstitute and regroup themselves, and although they may even be manipulated by managers and incorporated into the superstructured organizations, their social impact is very

---

* In the Communist countries, where, as a result of the abolition of private ownership of the means of production, bureaucratic power is even more centralized than in the Western democracies, this is a leading topic of criticism. See Günther Hillmann: *Selbstkritik des Kommunismus* (Hamburg; 1967).

modest compared with that of the mammoth organizations superimposed upon them. Bureaucratization completes a structural change in society which affects every single individual. But its most important consequence is a drastic change in the work style of human beings, a change which in turn has changed the human attitude toward work.

Since the manual and industrial trades have always been a masculine domain, the masculine way of life is obviously the first to be affected by these changes. Man's scope for initiative in work is considerably restricted, and this upsets his relationship to his work. Practically, intellectually, and emotionally he is forced to reorient himself to his working life—a process which extends deep into the core of his being. Obviously work has been made immensely easier, and much less demanding physically, by the increasing perfection of technology. Innumerable processes have been completely taken over by machines, while others have been considerably simplified by partial mechanization. Many jobs that formerly could only be performed standing up can now be done sitting down. Working hours have been reduced, and our whole work culture is geared to convenience. All in all, work itself can be said to force people into passivity.

Of course this is not true of all occupations. Mining and the metal and construction industries still involve heavy, dangerous labor, although they too employ many labor-saving devices. Pneumatic tools, conveyor belts, steam shovels, cranes, automatic and semi-automatic machines of all kinds make things easier for the working man; nevertheless, something of the risky, active quality of the old-time working life survives. Work of this kind, however, is being overshadowed by secondary activities. On today's vast construction sites or in a huge modern smelting works, a handful of men can be seen doing the really dangerous labor with the help of tremendous machines, while a labyrinthine administrative force carries on behind the scenes. Research studies confirm that far more people are engaged in secondary and tertiary areas of work than in primary ones. This trend parallels the trend in soldiering in which combat troops are steadily reduced, while the bureaucracy and the auxiliary forces expand. Even work in the primary areas is becoming a one-sided functional specialization requiring little personal initiative and no real development of all-round capacities. What is needed is technological adaptation to working conditions dictated by the superstructure. The working man becomes, as Stalin once put it, a little cog in the machine, insignificant, anonymous, a bit of human fuel for the supermachine of industrial culture, just as the soldier of today is merely cannon fodder for the machinery of war.

The starting point of all Karl Marx's theories was the idea of an "unalienated mankind," of the "true nature" of man. His desire to liberate the proletariat and overthrow capitalism is rooted in the notion of a universal humanity. The concept of the "total man," which is referred to again and again in Marx's writing, forms the basis of his criticism of industrial society organized on the principle of the division of labor. He believed that industrial labor provides no opportunity for self-fulfillment, that it does not permit man to run his own life and so he cannot escape from the

144

specific, exclusive sphere of activity which is forced upon him. Marx wanted every man to enter fully into his work, affirming himself in it and being affirmed by others.

By "man" Marx means the male: he writes about hunters, fishermen, and shepherds, or critics and artists, and he sees these occupations as masculine domains. In *Das Kapital* and other works he often mentions Robinson Crusoe, speaking of that voyager's "bright island." Although Marx rejects Robinson Crusoe-type utopias, he describes Crusoe and his versatile activities with great sympathy. Indeed, the wholeness of Robinson Crusoe's existence, which might be called the life of a universal male—hunter, fisherman, farmer, shepherd, toolmaker, carpenter, and so on, all in one—accounts for the attraction this figure holds for readers who themselves are subject to the ever more radical specialization of the industrial age.

Specialization of labor began early in history: men separated into groups of hunters, craftsmen, traders, medicine men, and chiefs, for instance. But each of these special skills provided a universally human existence with its own purposes and its own fulfillment. Certain archetypal occupations, despite their specialization, still offer the male scope for all-round development by drawing on many different human qualities. Farmer, blacksmith, hunter, soldier, priest, physician, mason, builder, trader—all these primeval occupations retain some contact with the "whole man." Up to the industrial revolution there were at most a few dozen occupations; since then the occupational catalog has expanded to include tens of thousands of specialized jobs, most of which challenge only a minute fraction of the qualities inherent in human nature.

The increase of abstract specialization and functionalization in secondary and tertiary occupations is shown most strikingly by the constantly growing number of salaried employees or white-collar workers. They are in fact the only social group that is still growing; all others, particularly the self-employed, are decreasing. In 1882 there were 300,000 salaried employees in Germany; in 1925 there were 3,500,-000; by 1961 they had increased to 5,850,000. Between 1932 and 1958 the proportion of white-collar workers and civil servants in the total working population rose from 18 to 26 per cent. In Austria between 1934 and 1951 the percentage rose from 21.5 to 32 per cent. Among the non-self-employed workers of all industrialized countries the center of gravity is shifting from laborers to white-collar workers. This trend is particularly noticeable in large cities, especially in the United States, where, as early as 1929, 42 per cent of all people in the labor force were salaried or white-collar employees. By 1966, over 70 per cent were white-collar workers.

What exactly are white-collar workers? The question is not easy to answer; there are many contradictory ideas and mutually exclusive theories. Bourgeois theorists tend to regard them as a new middle class which is becoming steadily stronger and will eventually put an end to the old class society. Many of these theorists believe that white-collar workers are "expanding into entrepreneurial functions," and "taking the wheel of the economy." Siegfried Aufhäuser says: "If we compare a company to a ship, the white-collar workers function not as captain but as first mates, ship's officers, and engineers. Seamen and officers form a community exposed to common risks. Workers and staffers ought to recognize that their lives are interlinked in a similar way."[23] This is a highly romanticized view, however; the middle-class theory applies only to certain cultural behavior patterns among white-collar workers. And if we take participation in general prosperity and consumption as a criterion, large segments of the working class also belong to the "middle stratum." The lumping together of all salaried employees as "ship's officers" disregards the fact that few of them have more entrepreneurial power and better chances of advancement than the average worker.

For this reason Ludwig Neundörfer goes so far as to describe staff employees as slaves of the economy who are even less independent than the workers. "The white-collar worker is the slave of a system of technologically advanced big business in a sense far beyond the mere exploitation of his labor and the refusal to pay a fair wage for it. He is controlled, even in his most private domains, by the will of those anonymous powers whose visible representatives stand on the top rungs of his own ladder, who are 'employees' like himself, but only in the legal, not the sociological, sense. He is told what to do and how to do it." In support of this Neundörfer cites the thesis of Siegfried Kracauer that the white-collar workers are actually "the masses." "They are

147

the human product of a rationalized supereconomy. Even more than the workers they are functionalized, rationalized people."[24]

The conservative school of Marxists, committed to the old two-class model and hence to the principle of "working-class unity," concentrates on the white-collar workers' status as employees and says that any authority they have is delegated to them from above by the employer, subject to countermand. Thus they become buffers between capital and labor and in extreme cases even a *Lumpenbourgeoisie*. This school exposes as a myth the theory that the white-collar workers are "at the wheel of the economy" and says that the only real difference in the social situation of workers and salaried employees is that there are low-, medium-, higher-, and top-grade employees but no such distinctions among workers. Yet skilled workers and low-grade salaried employees are by no means on an equal level. A writer who changes professions and becomes a streetcar conductor is not improving his status, any more than a carpenter who becomes an office worker. But a locksmith who becomes a foreman immediately acquires medium-grade employee status, so that he outranks not only the men under him in the shop but also his staff of payroll clerks, draftsmen, and stock clerks. And while these office workers normally remain in the same occupation, the foreman may go on to become an engineer, plant superintendent, or manager. He gets to take the "wheel of the economy" not by virtue of his staff function but as a technological specialist. I personally know more laborers than low-grade salaried employees who have succeeded in working their way into the hierarchical chain of command or even opening their own businesses without going through the institutionalized channels of advancement.

The function theory seems to offer the most realistic definition of the white-collar worker. It attempts to classify and group jobs according to the scope of their duties within the division of labor in industrial society. Four main functions can be identified: administrative, interpretive and analytical, managerial, and merchandising. Thus from the viewpoint of the fundamentally democratized modern industrial society, the various types of staff employee are classified in an apparently value-free system. According to this theory they do not stand above working-class production workers of equal status and rights, but on the same level.

Although the function theorists try to avoid any connection with theories of social stratification and power, they say that the salaried employee has better prospects of advancement than the worker. Fritz Croner, a leading sociologist in this field, has even come to the sociologically peculiar conclusion that white-collar workers constitute a "functional group with superior learning motivation." While he rejects an undemocratic stratification of society by class, he is finally driven to describe them as "an open-ended social stratum," which constitutes an entity because of its "sense of solidarity with all staff employees regardless of their salary level and function." He speaks of the "obvious evidence of this sense of solidarity" displayed by white-collar workers in all countries of the industrialized West. Their sense of solidarity "expresses the common social situation of all white-collar workers without regard to salary, position, or quality of work—their awareness of the fact that their chances in life are determined by their functions."[25] This is completely false. What does Croner mean by "chances in life"? Clearly he means chances of advancement. But what kind of position can the office boy or low-grade civil servant attain that is not also attainable by a skilled worker?

The actual difference between the top and the bottom of Croner's "one class" of salaried employees is enormous. In the companies Neundörfer studied, the salaries of 1.8 per cent of all employees were 500 per cent of the average, while those of 88.6 per cent ranged between 50 and 200 per cent of the average. The difference becomes even more striking when we consider the impossibility of crossing the gulf between the lower and the upper grades. Advancement channels are strictly institutionalized, and the top positions are attainable only by way of specialized training and university education. These positions are filled by people selected and trained for them from the outset—that is, by technical school and college graduates, who compose 7.7 per cent and 3.2 per cent, respectively, of all employees. The rest spend their lives doing jobs which, in the case of 30.5 per cent of the men and 86.3 per cent of the women, cannot be classified as either specialized or semiskilled.[26]

Office work is organized like production work. "It is 'functionalized' under 'professional discipline' for its technical purposes. This leaves a huge residue of routine jobs which serve only to keep the bureaucratic information machine running, while independent responsibility is reduced to a 'function' within a system and the 'intellectual potency' of labor—labor as an avocation—is reduced to a minimum and concentrated in the hands of certain specialists or in the upper ranges of the 'hierarchy.' "[27] Fritz Below is right in saying that only the concept of the "managerial employee" is unequivocal; according to the particular nature of their jobs, there is a bigger gap between the top employees and the others than between workers and salaried employees. Thus there exists at the top of the bureaucracy an exclusive power elite into which an average salaried employee has as little chance of penetrating as a blue-collar worker. And there are lower-ranking white-collar groups whose social and economic status is no higher—and may be lower—than that of most skilled workers. While the workers, like the intellectuals, are still in a position to rebel against bureaucracy, the white-collar masses, as Braun rightly points out, have been subjugated by it. The function theory fails in its analysis because it holds to a purist democratic social model, regardless of fact. Instead of admitting that the "employee class" is divided according to an obvious status system in order to bare the interaction of function and status, it masks the new differences of rank and thus even blurs the functions.

Ralf Dahrendorf, on the other hand, proposes a vertical differentiation of the white-collar class into regular employees, experts, and bureaucrats. Nevertheless, he insists on its unity as a "service class," defined by its relationship of service to authority and by its membership in the "ruling class," since it exercises certain forms of delegated authority. This, however, holds only theoretically with regard to the historical derivation of employee functions from entrepreneurial functions. In reality, any authority ever inherent in most low-grade white-collar positions has vanished, while the high-level positions are becoming in practice nearly autonomous forms of authority.

Actually, in all modern industrialized countries we are approaching the almost total bureaucratization which Max Weber predicted as a possible future development, although he thought it had not yet materialized in his time. In a nightmare vision he foresaw how unfree workers and employees might some day be in a universal bureaucracy.

¶ Since every power struggle with a state bureaucracy is hopeless and since there is no appeal to an agency which as a matter of principle would be interested in limiting the employer's power. . . . Who would want to deny that such a potentiality lies in the womb of the future? . . . Let us assume for the moment that this possibility were our "inescapable" fate: who would then not smile about the fear of our literati that the political and social development might bring us *too much* "individualism" or "democracy" or other such-like things, and about their anticipation that "true freedom" will light up only when the present "anarchy" of economic production and the "party machinations" of our parliaments will be abolished in favor of social "order" and "organic stratification"—that means, in favor of the pacifism of social impotence under the tutelage of the only really inescapable power: the bureaucracy in state and economy?[28]

Doesn't the tremendous growth of bureaucratic machinery show that we are close to such a state of affairs? Yet according to a theory recently propounded by progressive Marxists, this growth indicates that the class society is about to be superseded by the classless society. Günther Hillmann has spoken of bureaucracy's "dual nature" in that it is the last remaining class and at the same time no longer a class at all. This is proved, he says, by the steady expansion of bureaucracy, for although it already possesses monopolistic power over information and decision making, it is forced to enlist and collaborate with more and more specialists of all kinds. Such an expansion indicates that as a class, it is open at the bottom and hence is beginning to disintegrate. Bureaucracy is no longer a class because all its functionaries and even the outsiders are now subject to the "quasi-automatic apparatus." There is no longer any one man, even at the center of the apparatus, who could be said to control it. Obviously Hillmann's theory has a tinge of wishful thinking, since the new social elite which is coming to manipulate society as a whole in the interests of this automatic apparatus is not really democratized by bringing in experts from outside. How that process is supposed to lead to real democratization is not clear, for advisers do not challenge but merely slightly expand the established power of the bureaucracy.

The so-called unity of the white-collar stratum merely serves to mask bureaucracy's real power structure; it is a camouflage for the new class. The purpose of this camouflage is evident: the artificially produced false consciousness of a single "employee class" is supposed to keep all lower-grade employees starting with the office boy solidly lined up with the top bureaucrats. The lower employees provide a democratic façade for the extraordinary power wielded by the holders of a few top positions over economic, political, and cultural affairs. Such a form of "democratization" is a quite unconvincing fiction, wholly dependent upon a false "employee solidarity" artificially maintained. For its part, the Communist bloc claims that the bureaucratic elite represents not the usurpation of power by a new ruling class, but the whole nation's desire for a "classless society." This is at best a pious self-deception.

It is conceivable that the vast majority if not all of the working population will someday become salaried employees. Other forces in addition to the growth of bureaucracy are steering society in this direction; one is that many politicians believe it desirable, for social-political reasons, to make more and more groups of workers salaried employees under the law. When this trend, which is being hastened by automation, reaches its end, there will be no more workers but merely a society consisting solely of employees. To assume that it will necessarily be a democratic society would be utopian.

Another social phenomenon closely connected with the constant increase in the number of white-collar workers is the constant decrease in the number of the self-employed. In Germany the percentage of the self-employed people

fell from 38 per cent in 1882 to 21 per cent in 1925 and to
13 per cent in 1958. All highly industrialized countries show
a similar decrease. The comparable figures for the United
States are 40.4 per cent in 1870; 27.1 per cent in 1910; 13.3
per cent in 1954 (Croner's figures). Occupations that offer
scope for enterprise are becoming less numerous. On the
average, people are better off economically, but they are
losing their economic initiative. Nonindependent work is
also changing its character; it grows easier, it loses in significance and becomes more abstract. Personal responsibility is
reduced to minute segments of a gigantic production complex which most individuals cannot begin to visualize. In
return for these sacrifices, as it were, bureaucratic industrial
society to some extent guarantees earnings and recognizes
the employee's greater claims on society. In addition, the
white-collar worker is offered the sop of a false sense of
heightened occupational prestige. It is hardly surprising that
in this situation the concept of work, especially man's work,
as a calling, as the ideal of an active, fulfilled life, should fall
into disrepute and that people should become consumption-
rather than production-minded. As work becomes less independent and thus less capable of arousing a feeling of
achievement, it becomes devalued.

The new upper class of top bureaucrats does not appropriate property and other assets as the classic "capitalist
class" did; rather, it appropriates social activism. The two
classes of the bureaucracy might well be called the active
and the deactivated. The former have seized for themselves
the satisfying social and economic activities, while the rest

must be content with the standardized routine jobs which require no real initiative and no psychological independence. The result is that the few members of the active class are often so busy that they can hardly catch their breath. They gladly work eighteen hours a day and often voluntarily go without vacations and recreation, while the many members of the deactivated class are forced almost completely into leisure-time modes of behavior. Since the latter's work holds no interest for them, even the considerably reduced work-week is still too long. The former are the "doers," the people who plan and think ahead, who make decisions, get things going, supervise and reorganize; the others must be content with passively adapting themselves. And anyone who does not adapt, anyone who demands an active role, winds up as an outsider, unless he has the prerequisites for promotion to the upper class.

I have shown that the course of events seems to have made the traditional male role untenable in two decisive areas of masculine self-fulfillment: fighting and work. Whatever explanation of man's historical concept of himself we may subscribe to—whether we believe it is determined by the times and hence is subject to change, or whether we feel it was naturally given—the fact is that the traditional versions of the male role, which are still important as formative images, are no longer relevant to his situation. Neither defiant behavior nor an active working life can be regarded today as a generally fulfillable norm. This discrepancy between the images of "all-round masculinity" and the possibilities that contemporary society provides is responsible for the impotent rage and the absurdist revolt described earlier in this book.

On the other hand, woman's sexual role, which assigns her the task of conceiving, bearing, and feeding children, is itself a "fully human specialization" which, far from conflicting with her female existence, brings it to fulfillment. Man's full humanity is not safeguarded in this way, which is the reason why the ideal of all-round humanity is pre-eminently a male one. From the beginning of human history man's role specializations have been far more numerous and differentiated than woman's. Woman is naturally more engrossed in her sexual specialization: she is virgin, beloved, wife, mother, grandmother. The male analogue is not his evolution from youth to grandfather but the development of his specialized roles as soldier, worker, craftsman, leader, priest, intellectual, artist, and his "rise" from the lowest ranks within these specializations to higher ones. Women are closer to their archetype than men and are therefore more like one another than men can ever be. (For this reason it is always more plausible in life as well as in fairy tales, that a man of the highest rank should marry a woman from the lowest than vice versa.) Woman never needs to struggle so hard to achieve full humanity as man does; consciously or unconsciously she bears it within her. Hence she does not need to build up complicated ideals concerning her role in the world and is in a better position to adapt to social and economic changes. As Margaret Mead says, for women to

achieve a sense of irreversible achievement "it is only necessary that they be permitted by the given social arrangements
to fulfill their biological role. . . . If men are ever to be at
peace, ever certain that their lives have been lived as they
were meant to be, they must have, in addition to paternity,
culturally elaborated forms of expression that are lasting and
sure."[29]

What is to become of the traditional masculine qualities which the male has been putting to use for thousands of
years? Can he retrain himself? Can a new, universally acceptable model be created for nonactive, nonfighting male
behavior? Or can we invent models for some type of active,
fighting behavior that will be justifiable and meaningful in
our present life context? Some signs already seem to point
in this direction. The sportsman or playboy type, or sometimes a combination of the two, is already almost universally
recognized. But will images of this kind suffice? To answer,
we must determine to what extent the male attributes of
enterprise and fighting spirit are acquired and to what extent they are innate.

If we restrict the term aggression to so-called "intraspecific aggression," that is to say, to aggressive actions
toward members of one's own species, the matter of keeping
it within tolerable social limits seems relatively simple. Regardless of whether we consider such behavior instinctive
or acquired, it can be relatively easily discouraged socially
and could be largely eliminated through prohibitions and
training. But aggressiveness is not so neatly delimited; aggressive human behavior is made up of many components.

A general creative urge, self-assertion, a striving for independence or expansion, affective outbursts—all these may contribute to it, as may intellectual drives prompted by ethical or religious ideas. In principle the possibility of aggressive behavior is inherent in all active and voluntary behavior. Conversely it follows that active behavior of any kind at all harbors a germ of aggression, that every kind of activism contains an aggressive element. This means that aggression and activism are identical so far as their origins go. Only our subjective evaluation of our own or other people's activism brands it as aggressive or nonaggressive. Thus an army officer may describe his own military and political attitude as completely nonaggressive while characterizing as aggressive an antiwar demonstration by pacifists using purely passive methods.

This means that if we take it to the extreme, there really is such a thing as "pacifist aggression"; there is even a purely passive mode of behavior that becomes aggression. Aggression is extremely convertible. The restriction of the term to deliberately hostile actions or to the use of force in assault and killing creates a false perspective. Aggression is not just forceful, bellicose behavior but any encroachment on or interference with other people's domains, any form of pushing or refusing to give way, any seizure of objects to which one has no legal right. A neighbor may take it as aggression if my son climbs over his fence to retrieve a ball that has landed in his garden. I may take it as aggression if a neighbor keeps the volume of his television set turned too high. One man may take it as aggression if another refuses to let him board a bus ahead of him. Or a foreman may brusquely reject a workman's suggestion because he regards it as an infringement of his own rights. Even the glance with which one person sizes up another can be interpreted as aggression. A casual remark, a smile, stepping into an unfamiliar street, conciliatory intervention in a conflict between other people, wearing a red tie, overtaking another car—all these can be aggressive acts. It makes no difference whether the action is intended aggressively; what matters is whether the other person interprets it as aggression or not.

All activism of any kind, and especially activism in business and professional life, somehow involves aggression toward somebody and will certainly be interpreted as such by somebody or other. The more our world becomes an open world and the greater the population density and the crowding, the truer this becomes. These processes increase our subjective readiness to interpret any active behavior by other people as aggressive. But at the same time our readiness to discharge our frustrated desire for activism in acts of aggression is also increased, so that activism is transformed into aggression.

Thus aggression may be regarded as a medium of expression for activism and consequently is almost impossible to control completely. It is capable of disguising and transforming itself so radically that the aggressor himself may be largely or entirely unaware of its true nature. Communists consider themselves justified in instigating aggression within society (i.e., civil wars) while maintaining that aggression as a form of foreign policy (i.e., wars of conquest against other nations) is inadmissible. Their own aggressiveness in foreign affairs takes on the cloak of solidarity with the oppressed rebels in other countries. Likewise are not the "hawks," the militant wing in American foreign policy masking genuinely aggressive intentions with the pretext of honoring an alliance with governments which are rejected by their own peoples?

If political acts of aggression can take cover behind ideals or legal pretexts and excuses so that they become unrecognizable to the aggressor's own consciousness, how much easier it is for aggression to disguise itself in personal relationships, which are so much more intricate and complex. Scholarly criticism, for example, a well-known form of intellectual sublimation, is likely to be experienced as aggression by those who are being criticized. Aggressive behavior in medicine, seldom recognized as such, is discernible wherever the patient becomes the object of medical research; it is particularly obvious in surgical interventions. Aggression is rampant in the field of law: legislation, interpretation of the law, and the administration of law and justice have frequently been marked by violent hostility, however disguised behind legal formulas.

Scientists have still not been able to determine whether aggressive modes of behavior express an elemental need inherent in human nature or whether this need is merely a product of false education and harmful environmental influences. Comparative ethology (the science of animal behavior) and *behavioral psychology* are diametrically opposed. The former assumes that man's behavior, like that of animals, is determined by more or less strong instincts; the latter maintains that man is absolutely without instincts and must learn all his patterns of behavior. Behavioral psychology describes man's fundamental behavior as "operative," meaning that it is not a response to external stimuli but itself influences the environment and is either reinforced or frustrated (or "negatively reinforced") by the reactions of the environment. It is called *operative* in contrast to *reactive* because reactive behavior is governed by the vegetative nervous system and is involuntary, while operative behavior seems to be dictated by the central nervous system and hence by the human will. Fundamentally such an interpretation too rests on the assumption that man is by nature an active being. According to this theory the connecting link between activism and aggression is frustration. When operative—i.e., active—behavior is frustrated and man's psychic equilibrium is disturbed, the reaction is aggression, which is merely an attempt to compensate for the disturbance.[30]

The social psychologist Alexander Mitscherlich puts it even more simply: "Forced renunciation breeds hostility." Basically he looks at it somewhat differently from the behavioral psychologists, as do all scholars influenced by Freud's psychoanalytic theory. He shows that society imposes libidinal sacrifices upon the individual and that this results in "surplus aggressive libido." For this reason society provides outlets through which the individual can express his hostilities.[31] The main task of social education is to convert aggressive libidinal desires into socially useful activity. This school of thought therefore regards aggressive modes of behavior as "neurotic reconversions of activism into aggressiveness."

The behaviorists of the Darwinian evolutionary school are the most radical champions of the aggressive instinct. They regard it as a primary, species-preserving instinct which creates an inalienable basis for a great many important, useful, and admirable human qualities such as love, friendship, and enthusiasm. Of course, they also recognize that it is precisely the instinctive nature of the aggressive urge that makes it so dangerous. In his book *On Aggression* Konrad Lorenz, one of the outstanding representatives of this school, defends the instinctual nature of aggression against those who deny it: "It is the spontaneity of the instinct that makes it so dangerous. If it were merely a reaction to certain external factors, as many sociologists and psychologists maintain, the state of mankind would not be as perilous as it really is."[32]

So far as the present study goes, we need not subscribe unconditionally to either of these theories concerning the origin of aggression. The point is that essentially active human behavior is remarkably close to all aggressive patterns of conduct. Both these schools agree that aggressive behavior, whatever its ultimate causes, is in fact unavoidable. Whether the need for hostility is innate or is produced by frustration appears of little importance compared with the fact that it is present in every individual, however vigorously he may reject and deny it. Without doubt both aggression-promoting and aggression-impeding factors are present in the structure of society and in the ideals a culture upholds. As yet, however, no form of society or culture has succeeded

THE MALE IN CRISIS

in eliminating aggression altogether. To try to change the social and cultural conditions responsible for aggression is to produce fresh aggression, for history shows that all great ideals and notions of everlasting peace among men have led to new conflicts and wars as soon as the time came to implement them. Lorenz believes that humanity is not warlike and aggressive *because* it is split into parties hostile to one another, but that this particular structuring provides the stimulus situation essential for the discharge of social aggression. Here he quotes the biologist Erich von Holst: "If ever a doctrine of universal salvation should gain ascendancy over the whole earth . . . it would at once divide into two strongly opposing factions (one's own true one and the other heretical one) and hostility and war would thrive as before, mankind being—unfortunately—what it is!"[33]

There is an internal phenomenon in society which justifies this statement: our general attitude toward criminals. History has hardly known a form of society in which criminals did not exist. Scientists have puzzled over this and come up with all kinds of explanations: hereditary tendencies, physical and psychological anomalies, economic deprivation—and even the rising standard of living which, according to some authorities, leads to "affluent criminality." Yet none of the comparative studies of the tendencies and circumstances of criminals and noncriminals have uncovered significant differences between them. In the last few decades, however, the findings of social psychology have indicated that society creates its own criminals in order to abreact its own aggressive tendencies against them. Society needs criminals for its growth and survival. As Sepp Schindler says, the criminal actions of the minority serve to reassure and exonerate the majority that likes to believe itself superior. Numerous studies have found evidence that criminals are not born but made within certain sociodynamic situations. A juvenile who happens to get into trouble with the law is forced by social censure to begin thinking of himself as a "criminal." The less secure his relations to society are, the more easily he will submit to this label. He is soon shunted into groups of other delinquents whose aggression turns against the society that is treating them in an aggressive manner. They thus become the scapegoats of society.

James Dollard and a team of American scholars suggest that the evolution of criminal justice demonstrates a process of universal significance: a shifting of aggression in order to utilize it for social purposes. This reveals a great deal about the process whereby a larger society, especially a national one, is formed. A society can arise only if the majority succeed in suppressing and repressing its aggressive impulses to a certain extent. The members of a society always have feelings of hostility which threaten its survival. Society's first way of controlling this dangerous level of aggression is to deflect it outward through wars, colonizing ventures, and so forth. But the measure of aggression is too great to be discharged in this way. Some continuous process is needed, and the answer is to turn aggression against the criminal. The man who has had to give up blood vengeance and private feuds satisfies his need for revenge and retaliation in the collective act of criminal justice, in which originally every man actually played his part (as in punishment by stoning). He succeeds in suppressing his own criminal desires, but only by joining in a collective action to project them onto the criminal. According to Raoul Schindler, group dynamics can only be created and maintained by means of a scapegoat, and hence a society's dynamics can be explained in terms of the availability of scapegoats. Thus Sepp Schindler writes that society needs not only common goals but also universally accepted objects of aggression. Only so long as it can keep this dynamic constant is its own constancy guaranteed. While he states unequivocally that society creates its own criminals because it needs them, Schindler finally asks very dubiously whether any socio-dynamic situation exists in which a society without "criminals" is possible.

The inescapable conclusion is that if man succeeds—as he must succeed unless he wants to blow the world apart—in more or less denying himself foreign political aggression, then aggression within society will increase almost automatically. Among the many indications of the direction events may take is the fact that in the United States during this century 750,000 people have already been murdered.[34] Of course the trend toward intersociety aggression will not necessarily be confined to an increase in criminality. Pent-up activism and aggressiveness may express itself in other forms: aggressive driving on the highway, for instance. In what might more accurately be called "the battle of the highways," the monthly number of traffic victims in a country such as Germany equals an army regiment.

What are we to do with surplus activism and aggression? Members of the biological school of behavioral research have suggested that we should breed people who are relatively or entirely free from aggression. If we assume that instincts are inherited, this seems scientifically possible up to a certain point. By preventing aggressive people from reproducing, and confining the privilege of perpetuating themselves to the inaggressive we might create a peaceful human race. But it would take a very long time, and who knows what may happen before then? Not to mention the fact that the aggressive people would resist. To implement such a program would require a police state more monstrous than any that has ever existed. And what a lot of aggression it would take! Besides, even if we did succeed in letting the hawks die out and breeding nothing but doves, would the result be desirable? Wouldn't a society free from tensions lose all its dynamism? Or would completely new forms of aggressiveness emerge?

The alternative is the way of education. Here, as modern theories of learning have shown, the prospects are good, but unfortunately only on a long-term basis. We do not have centuries to deal with this problem; with regard to the opening up of the globe and man's mastery of it, the human race is in a crisis situation. If catastrophes on a gigantic scale are to be avoided, decisions must be taken soon. Catastrophe cannot be averted by warnings and moral lectures alone, nor by some verbal formula that will suppress the term "aggressiveness" and thereby give aggressiveness itself the freedom to assume any form it pleases, including even the guise of peacefulness.

Instead of denying aggression, we would do well to acknowledge that it is always present, regardless of circumstances, in every individual and in all human societies, emerging now from hypocritical masks, now in positive sublimation. We should therefore recognize that conscious control over it must continually be re-established. We can create outlet zones for aggression within society, perhaps by making contact sports a compulsory part of education, perhaps by reintroducing some new version of chivalrous dueling. Even better, we can encourage the arts that serve to abreact aggression or to purge us of it in the sense of the Greek catharsis. We can prescribe hallucinants to relax people, or agree to wage small "safety-valve" wars occasionally in remote areas such as the Antarctic. Such proposals have already been made. But will they be enough?

In my opinion there is only one course to take: the way of universal awareness, of deepening and widening our knowledge of the laws of human nature and human coexistence. This means better schools and educational opportunities for our children; it means educating the educators; above all, it means self-education, mass education in the widest sense with the help of the mass media—the universal self-enlightenment of mankind. The mass media will have to ask themselves whether they can in good conscience continue to gratify and simultaneously stimulate the unconscious aggressive tendencies of the masses. Unless they want to be accessories to catastrophe, they must decide to deepen their inherent potentiality for enlightenment and the dissemination of knowledge. But even enlightenment will not provide a final solution to the problem. A deeper common insight into the factors responsible for the human condition will be meaningful only if man acquires, together with his wider perception, a greater measure of responsibility, only if the authority due to a mature human being is restored to him as an individual. We have no option; there is no alternative to this course.

4

THE CRISIS
OF AUTHORITY

Those who carry the responsibility for making social decisions seem to have two options: to enlighten the people in order to make them more ready to do what their welfare requires or, toward the same objective, steadily to deprive them of all insight and abandon them to superficial stimuli and pleasures. But this view of the alternatives is based on a fallacy, for in the climate of industrial society it is not possible to keep all the people in a state of obedient dependence. Not even a council of hand-picked grand inquisitors familiar with every trick of psychology could make a society of this type permanently stable. It is true that great masses of people, perhaps even the majority, allow themselves to be misled and held in a state of psychological dependence by means of the trash fed to them by the press and the entertainment industry. But although it may be possible to keep many people in a state of blindly acquiescent dependence, it is impossible to subjugate all the people all the time. The reason is that besides the frustrating tendencies inherent in the laws of the superstructured society, this structure harbors a countervailing trend toward a democratic activation of man's claim to responsibility. The man who wants his due share of responsibility finds in industrial society a number of conditions that make it possible for him to attain it.

The most important of these conditions is the extensive democratization of knowledge. Industrial society is forced to keep numerous channels of education open to many people at all times in order to supply the necessary new talent and further equip those already employed for necessary reorganizations. Even elementary education today provides a greater amount of diversified knowledge than was available to the parent generation, a knowledge that is continually enriched even by the low-grade popular media. In principle, the accessibility of knowledge in all fields is granted by law; anyone may inform himself of anything, though in the Communist countries students, scientists, and technologists have often had to fight for such things as access to Western publications, lest the country fall behind intellectually. The more knowledge that becomes accessible even to the lower strata of society, the more human responsibility is fostered, leading to an increase in the number of people who not only feel entitled to make judgments about events and conditions but who also expect their judgments to carry some weight in society.

This brings us to the problem of authority, to which the final and most important chapter of this book addresses itself; most important because the solution of the other problems discussed hinges entirely upon the clarification of the problem of human authority. In Chapter II, "The Crisis of Eros," which outlined the external factors disturbing the male-female relationship in our time, it was stated that erotic relations suffer from disturbances originating elsewhere, namely in the areas of social activism and aggression. It was pointed out that socio-economic conditions tend to inhibit legitimate aggressive behavior and even to preclude it morally, so that the masculine drive toward active self-fulfillment is seriously restricted, if not totally suppressed. However, since present conditions are irreversible, this cannot be solved by reopening normal channels for aggressive activity.

And so we come to the area which I believe to be the only one where the problem can be solved: the most inward, crucial sphere of male existence, the sphere of authority. Authority as a social phenomenon is a male affair. Not that woman is—or should be—excluded from participating in it or exercising it, but her need for and conception of authority are less clearly defined and differently accentuated. Like the female activist urge, woman's attitude toward authority seems to be·more closely linked with direct biological processes than with the social ones and hence does not of itself develop the graduated, complex status structures of the man-made social system. Thus wherever and whenever authority is under discussion, the male himself is under discussion.

We must now ask what we mean by authority. Democratic society discredits this word and would like to drop it from the vocabulary, as it would the word "aggression." When used, "authority" is nearly always meant in a negative

173

sense. The word always has overtones of the threat of the authoritarian state, of political authority invoking higher powers, and of the "charismatic" posturing of the authority emanating from personalities. All too recently we have learned something about authoritarian states and leaders who arrogated to themselves the responsibility for all members of a society and presumed to make their decisions for them, including that of survival or extinction. But this ominous implication of the word distorts the vision of those who reject authority in any form. Here is a dilemma which has its comical side: one can be anti-authoritarian for authoritarian reasons! Only somebody who possesses or claims authority can fight against authorities of other kinds. Nothing requires more authority than Kant's demand that we should never blindly obey the command of authority and indeed should not even blindly subject ourselves to a superhuman authority as a moral lawgiver. This is why Kant added that man's conscience should be his only authority. If we are unwilling to submit to other authorities, it follows that we consider ourselves authorities. Kant's theory of the autonomy of man is concerned with this authority of the individual; it points to the democratic authority of the mature man, to authority by virtue of intelligence. Thus if we eliminate the whole concept of authority from our thinking just because we object to other people's arrogation of authority, we are making a mistake. We are in fact contesting something we claim for ourselves. We are trying, as it were, to pull up by the roots a tree which we only want to chop down.

This becomes obvious if we look at the etymological meaning of the term. *Authority* comes from the Latin word *auctoritas*, which in turn comes from *auctor*, a derivative of *augere*. *Augere* means to multiply, increase, allow to grow, and also to promote. Theodor Eschenburg shows how the concept has changed over the centuries while retaining something of its seminal Roman meaning. "*Auctoritas* induced people to conform voluntarily to another person's helpful counsel because they had confidence in his cogent superiority. One person authorizes another to give him counsel. The authorization implies freedom of decision. . . . The counsel of *auctoritas* is not an order, but its effect is that of an order. Among the essential characteristics of *auctoritas* is that it counsels helpfully and hence selflessly."[1]

Discussing the contemporary use of the term to denote man's relation to the authority of the state, Eschenburg's definition of authority is "inwardly accepted dependence as the occasion warrants it." This side of authority, subordination to other people's authority, should never lead us to forget that for the mature man, political authority cannot exist without his own free decision and consent. The mature man is in principle a free, authoritative being. Not by chance does the literature of the Communist New Left emphasize this fact. And for all the recent heated denials by the highest Catholic authority that the Church is a democracy, even Catholic theologians can now see Christianity as a force that can liberate man for mature responsibility.

Democracy's declared intention and highest aim is to permit every individual's personal authority to develop to the full and assert itself in the general political will. Democracy desires self-responsibility for all free citizens. This is an ideal, of course. While the ideal is embodied in some form in the laws of all states that can be called democratic, experience shows that it is extremely difficult to put into practice. Why? To answer, we must ask, what, basically, is the structure and distribution of authority in democratic industrial society, apart from political government? The fundamental governing principle in democracy is the principle of authority delegated from the bottom up. This is the essential difference between democracy and the authoritarian state, where authority exists only at the top and is delegated downward. In democracies, free citizens delegate parts of their personal authority to selected representatives, who exercise authority on their behalf in public life. In dictatorships, which is what we generally mean by "authoritarian" government, one authoritative personality or an elite group at the top delegates parts of its authority to people below in order that they may govern on its behalf.

But the authoritarian power system, antithetical to democracy though it is, has nevertheless penetrated the democratic system, where it persists in the form of bureaucratic government. Bureaucracy is the apparent successor of traditional patriarchal government and charismatic government centered in specific authoritarian personalities. Bureaucracy adapts itself to democratic society as a hierarchical structure of authority, and its elite groups have emerged as a new ruling class. Although, sociologically speaking, bureaucracy within a democratic state is not supposed to be anything more than an executive organ under full control of the citizens, in reality bureaucratic power has established itself as a secret system of government. It rules not by virtue of absolute authority, with power to command and to require obedience, but by means of its monopolistic control of the instruments which permit it to manipulate society. The authority of the rulers disappears behind the authority of the apparatus, so that the rulers can see themselves as the "servants" of those who are in fact ruled by them. But the authoritarian tendency of all bureaucracies is unmistakable, for all kinds of bureaucracy converge at the top and are often closely interconnected by a few individuals wearing many different hats. Typically, in most countries it is the party secretaries emerging from the party bureaucracy who hold or control the key governmental positions. This structure conflicts radically with the democratizing tendency of the industrial way of life.

Thus it seems that besides being faced with functional disturbances in his erotic relation to woman, frustration of his activism, and hindrances to the discharge of his normal aggressive tendencies, the male today is also threatened with losing his adult authority. In fact an ever-diminishing number of men now make ever more important decisions for an ever-increasing number of people. The specter conjured up by several writers in connection with the totalitarian state, the Big Brother who thinks, decides, and acts for everybody, is no mere fiction but a real threat, even in democratic countries. Nor does it improve matters when the Big Brothers, as represented by leadership groups and collectives, disappear behind the apparatus. They still decide more problems concerning more momentous issues than anyone has ever had to decide before. They intervene in every individual's personal life and even in the future of children yet unborn, and they can do this without having to assume full personal responsibility for their actions. For they themselves are subject to the law of the superstructure; at any time they can invoke the arbitrary power of the apparatus and retreat behind it. They can even invoke the will of the people, being either its elected representatives or appointees of those representatives. They have indeed a certain right to do so, because the rule of the apparatus is to some extent held in check and subject to review by the masses of democratic voters who go to the polls.

But is the rule of the apparatus really controlled by elections? Just how much attention do the public executive organs and the elite which controls the apparatus pay to the individual who is in process of becoming mature and responsible? Besides asking, as Eschenburg does, whether institutional authority is always exercised by legitimately appointed or chosen persons, we should ask how authority is actually distributed in our society. From the democratic standpoint, the answer can only be that it is distributed wrongly, unjustly, and therefore inadequately. Despite universal suffrage and the equality of all citizens under the law, despite the existence of a multitude of democratic institutions, the individual citizen's authority is by no means secure; on the contrary, he is being increasingly deprived of authority.

This is not entirely due to the authoritarian strivings of the people who control the superstructured social apparatuses; it is largely inherent in the way the apparatuses function. The people in control may be somewhat lacking in concern, in social scruples; but the majority of these people may well cherish democratic principles personally. They simply fail to realize that the enormous power in their hands and the organizational setup itself can lead them unaware into authoritarian behavior patterns to which they are in theory opposed. And they ignore the degree to which the ordinary citizen's power of decision is sapped by the very existence of the technological apparatuses. As a result new, hidden forms of authoritarian control emerge and rigidify within the formal democracy, wielding a totalitarian power much as in a dictatorship. The public has free speech but not much voice. It is kept busy with fictitious problems, diverted by demagoguery. Problems are settled by a few "experts," and questions and findings are so formulated that most citizens either cannot understand them at all or cannot help misunderstanding them. But even when the citizens do understand, even when they protest and demand a voice in the decision, authoritarian thinking overrides them if it has already made up its mind one way or the other.

This is particularly true of the financial and budgetary policies of governments today. Although these matters are undeniably complicated, it must be said that here facts are concealed and obscured on a scale which is not far short of totalitarianism. No democracy asks the citizen how much he is prepared to give his country and what is to be done with the money. As Max Weber remarked, no modern democratic industrial country has made parliament's most important function, the drawing up of the budget, the subject of a referendum. And since the ordinary citizen cannot in any case understand the rendering of accounts which the government submits to the legislature, those in charge can easily override the criticism of the few informed individuals who may present their opinions in the press. It is worth mentioning here that an extremely large percentage of government revenue is derived from indirect taxes, certainly the least equitable method of taxation and the hardest to keep a check on. In 1960 the Soviet Union began to abolish income tax based on earnings and to change over to a system of indirect taxation. All early socialists fought for exactly the opposite: the abolition of indirect taxation in favor of direct, progressive taxation determined by the level of income and open to public supervision. Yet whenever they came to power they failed to put this principle into practice. At the same time, the endless raising of income tax rates is most unfair and questionable, because it hampers capital accumulation and hence the economic independence of individual citizens. Thus in taxation too there is a tendency to rob the free citizen of more and more of his independence and responsibility.

Furthermore, as Parkinson's Law satirically puts it, a country's expenditure increases with its revenue. Every year the government appropriates more of the total national income and receives larger and larger sums to spend as it chooses. No platform in the world ever specifies how much money the party plans to spend to keep the promises made to the voters or where the money is to come from. A prime example is the United States, decried as the "stronghold of capitalism," where people were already saying twenty years ago that the only millionaire left was the government. As the economist Wilhelm Röpke said, all the citizen gets is pocket money to spend on modest pleasures such as football pools or television. The state is gradually offering to take charge of all his other needs, to relieve him of responsibility for all the elemental requirements of his life. Working and living conditions, arrangements for his children's education, and provision for his health and old age are increasingly determined by bureaucratic administrative decisions, thus depriving him of his independence and responsibility—a state of affairs radically opposed to democratic ideals.

One flagrant example from the host of problems this produces is the children's allowances which so many countries today "generously" award to families. From the economic standpoint such allowances are a pious fraud, at least under present conditions. Only a fraction of the taxes which a father actually pays for the raising of his children is refunded to him in the form of allowances, because half of everything he spends on his children goes back into the government's pocket in the form of direct or, above all, indirect taxes. Yet for the state, children are a long-term capital investment. As tomorrow's taxpayers, they will be paying the old age pensions of today's working population. Thus while fathers of families are in effect bearing the main burden of the state's economic and social programs, the state creates the impression that it is paying them a dole. Actually it is receiving a double return from them: high tax revenues, and children to guarantee its future. Every father of a larger than average family will testify that such practices give the public and his own children a false picture which invariably leads them to ask the snide question whether the family lives on the children's allowances alone. Even the father himself may find it difficult to explain the true situation—assuming that he understands it—and save face with his children.

This example of the undermining of man's authority by the state is particularly revealing because it concerns one of the principal responsibilities of the male: that of fatherhood. The father has to provide food and shelter, and it is his duty to mediate between his children and society. He stands for social morality; he makes moral demands on the child. These responsibilities are of the utmost importance not only for the adolescent but for the male himself, because his role of paternal authority reinforces his ego even as it requires him to grow and mature. As society takes over more and more family functions, however, parental authority in general is weakened, and the father's authority is abolished. The male is eclipsed as a father by the institutions of the "father state." And in the course of becoming invisible to the public eye and to the children he is raising, he becomes equally invisible to himself; the father role loses all validity for him; he does not need to take it seriously, since the state and society have in any case appropriated the most important attributes of fatherhood. The young are highly aware of this; hence the traditional father-son conflict exists today only in an attenuated form. Hatred of the father is being socialized. It turns away from the natural father to direct itself against the "father state."

The secret totalitarian authority of the bureaucratic apparatus destroys not only the authority of the father but also that of the responsible property owner and that of well-informed, perceptive, educated people, as well as the authority of achievement and old age. The bureaucracy hinders the free development of male authority in countless ways, prevents it from becoming effective in society, and shunts it into socially negligible "informal" areas. Only the minority who manage to work their way up the bureaucratic ladder to positions where the real power of decision begins ever experience the satisfaction of exercising authority.

In the crisis of male authority the democratic principle, although seemingly respected, is actually being reduced to a farce. How an idea can be turned into its opposite by dialectical reversal is clearly shown by the fact that even in the democratic countries, citizens who voice their democratic criticism are often called a threat to democracy. Anyone who dares to investigate structural sources of danger within democracy itself risks being branded as antidemocratic. Usually the first to cast stones are those who excel in exploiting the democratic ideal to obtain the privileges for themselves. People of this kind abound in the great bureaucratic apparatuses and their scientific auxiliaries. Since they tend to think that because they are in possession of social power they are also in possession of the truth, they are quick to stifle any criticism of existing conditions.

How can a solution be found for this crisis in the area of authority, where the disturbance in the masculine function is most acute if not most evident? The only promising answer lies in the fact that, while industrial development tends to promote bureaucratization, there is also a powerful countertrend toward democratization as accumulated knowledge becomes universally accessible. A self-renewing democratic activization is precisely what is needed to compensate for the irreversible loss man has suffered in the curtailment of his activism and his traditional opportunities for discharging aggression. We know that work activity will be curtailed still more and that aggression must be further reduced and controlled. The only real compensation for what man must sacrifice will be found not in complete withdrawal into leisure-time playing at activity and aggression, but in his acquiring an insight into the complex of contemporary society which will enable him to shoulder responsibility.

The modern industrial state is so constituted that nobody can assume and bear full responsibility for it. But we cannot continue to allow a few elite groups at the top to set themselves up as a "collective leadership" controlling all social authority. It is necessary to distribute authority as broadly as possible throughout society. Only a society that distributes the burden of authority widely will be able to get its constituents to act responsibly. To deprive a man of his authority is to make him irresponsible and cause him to act irresponsibly. The abstract "right to participate" is not enough; this right can be manipulated by the administrative apparatus. An authority is somebody who does not have to ask but who is himself asked and has to answer. Obviously a man who is merely allowed to vote in an election once every four years sees little sign of the responsibility due him as a mature man. He only sees himself being tricked by demagoguery and persuaded in more or less sophisticated ways to sanction by his vote what others have long ago done or decided. "The idea that a person's freedom consists in voting in elections and saying: 'Look, now I too have my one twenty-thousandth of a spokesman in our national blather institution' is one of the most ludicrous ideas in the world."[2] This sentence was written not by a Nazi or a Fascist but by Friedrich Engels, cofounder of Marxism. And it is pro-, not anti-, democratic, though in the sense of advocating an intensified democracy which does not treat constituents as "cattle driven to the polls."

The question of how democratization that leads to self-expression and -fulfillment can be achieved under present conditions seems to have only one feasible answer: it can be attained by utilizing man's elemental capacity to develop group activity. One of the remarkable and encouraging facts of our time is that while it favors the proliferation of superstructures in the form of powerful, all-encompassing, impersonal administrative bodies and complexes, an organizational principle opposed to the superstructure is beginning to play a major role in the thinking of social scientists.

The breakthrough came with the famous Hawthorne experiment carried out between 1927 and 1932 by Elton Mayo.[3] Experiments were conducted with a team of workers using a variety of technological methods to find out how performance could be improved. For a long time the experiments remained scientifically inconclusive because, although the team's productivity steadily increased, the factors responsible for the increase could not be identified. A force which eluded measurement by the social researchers improved production irrespective of changes in working conditions, pay, breaks, bonuses, etc. And even when all these incentives were withdrawn, the workers' productivity still rose. Only then did it become clear that the cause was not to be sought in the more comfortable seats, the breaks, the hot lunches, and the other benefits provided by the experimenters, but in the special group dynamics and the psychological attitude of the team members. One of the decisive factors was the psychological situation of the group, which felt honored that it was the focus of the researchers' attention. Another was its team spirit, and still another was the particular kind of informal contact between its members.

This experiment led psychologists into the methodical analysis of the communal life of small groups of people; the science of group dynamics had been born. This discipline investigates what holds a group together, how information and communication originate within a group, what inherent structure of authority it possesses, and what specifically produces motivation for cooperative action. It seems that every group has, besides its formal chief, its unofficial, informal leaders who are indispensable in maintaining contact between the members and who decisively influence joint action. It has been shown that in a group capable of action, everything is not under the control of a single leader; on the contrary, about five separate leadership functions can be distinguished: (1) the guidance function; (2) a mediating and ordering function, directed chiefly toward appropriate behavior within the group; (3) the exemplary function; (4) the teaching function; and (5) the function of moral support for the weaker members of the group. Insights of this kind have made the fundamental principles of communal social life identifiable. They show that man is a group being, and that all major social orders build up from group orders.

Thus if man can be democratically activated at all, it can only be from below, through the formation of primary groups. Only the development of group activity can combat the depersonalizing effects of the superstructures, for only in the group can there be a real growth of human authority within a clearly recognizable framework. Only the group can compensate for the individual's loss of public authority to the bureaucratic superstructures. Of course, now that the laws of group dynamics have been discovered, they are being enlisted in the service of the superstructure, which uses them for its own ends. But wherever group activity develops, even if it is manipulated at first, it will acquire influence over the broader forms of social organization. Group activity creates from below new authority structures which tend to extend their influence upward. From such a base the new structures of authority can grow to become part of multigroups and larger organizations.

This is the one real possibility of restoring male psychological capacity for action and authority on a maximum scale. And only by regaining authority can the male world overcome the other crises in the spheres of aggression, action, and Eros. This applies to the West as well as the East; democratic penetration of the superstructures is needed equally everywhere. In both worlds authority must be redistributed on a wider basis in order to restore the petrified machinery of government to flexibility and vigor by opening it up to group influence. It is by this means that the male can best resist the feminizing and infantilizing tendencies of the time. The only alternative to engaging in this struggle consciously is a kind of social suicide by default. It is what Kant was referring to when he said: "Immaturity [*Unmündigkeit*] is the inability to use one's reason without another person's guidance. This immaturity is one's own fault when it is caused not by a deficiency of reason but by a deficiency of resolution and courage to exercise that reason without relying on another person's guidance."[4]

NOTES

Chapter 1

1. Helmut Schelsky: *Soziologie der Sexualität* (Hamburg; 1955), p. 21.
2. Alexander Mitscherlich: *Auf dem Weg zur vaterlosen Gesellschaft* (Munich; 1965), p. 89.
3. *The New York Times* (August 10, 1969), p. 9.
4. Herbert von Borch: *The Unfinished Society* (Indianapolis: Bobbs-Merrill; 1962), p. 195.

Chapter 2

1. Helmut Schelsky: *Soziologie der Sexualität* (Hamburg; 1955), p. 104.
2. Karen Horney: *The Neurotic Personality of Our Time* (New York: Norton; 1937), p. 159.
3. Robert Musil: *The Man Without Qualities* (New York: Coward-McCann; 1953).
4. Ernst Jünger: *Der Kampf als inneres Erlebnis* (Berlin; 1926).
5. Ludwig Marcuse: "Einige Aufklärungen," in *Jahrbuch für kritische Aufklärung—Club Voltaire II* (Munich; 1965), pp. 12 *ff*.
6. Schelsky: *Soziologie der Sexualität*, p. 75.
7. Gottfried Benn: *Ausdruckswelt* (Wiesbaden; 1949).
8. *Christ in der Zeit*, Nos. 37–44 (1966).

9. Herbert von Borch: *The Unfinished Society* (Indianapolis: Bobbs-Merrill; 1962), p. 179.
10. Schelsky: *Soziologie der Sexualität*, p. 81.
11. Abram Kardiner: *Sex and Morality* (Indianapolis: Bobbs-Merrill; 1954).
12. Schelsky: *Soziologie der Sexualität*, p. 84.
13. Arnold Gehlen: *Sozialpsychologische Probleme in der industriellen Gesellschaft* (Hamburg; 1957), p. 42.
14. Alexander Mitscherlich: *Auf dem Weg zur vaterlosen Gesellschaft* (Munich; 1965), p. 456.
15. David Riesman: *The Lonely Crowd* (New York: Anchor Books; 1953), p. 69.
16. Margaret Mead: *Male and Female* (New York: Dell; 1949), pp. 278–9.
17. Ibid., p. 229.
18. Ibid., p. 283.

Chapter 3

1. Karl Reinhardt: *Die Krise des Helden* (Munich; 1962), p. 107.
2. Ibid., p. 108.
3. Herman Kahn: *On Escalation* (New York: Praeger; 1965).
4. V. D. Sokolovsky: *Military Strategy* (New York: Praeger; 1966).
5. Oskar Morgenstern: *The Question of National Defense* (New York: Random House; 1959), p. 295.
6. Ibid., p. 295.
7. Ibid., pp. 75–6.
8. Ibid., p. 296.
9. Hans-Georg von Studnitz: *Rettet die Bundeswehr* (Stuttgart; 1967).
10. Max Weber: *Economy and Society* (New York: Bedminster Press; 1968), III, 1393.
11. Morris Janowitz: *The Professional Soldier* (New York: Free Press; 1960), p. 42.

12. Helmut Schmidt: "Was fehlt der Bundeswehr" in Wolfram von Raven ed., *Armee gegen den Krieg* (Stuttgart: Degerloch; 1966), p. 104.
13. Janowitz: *The Professional Soldier*, pp. 31–2.
14. *Der Spiegel*, 38 (1966), p. 18.
15. Rolf R. Bigler: *Der einsame Soldat* (Frauenfeld; 1963), p. 53.
16. Ibid., p. 50.
17. Ibid., p. 16.
18. *Atomzeitalter*, 67 (1966), p. 214.
19. Reinhardt: *Der Krise des Helden*, p. 111.
20. *Merkur*, 187, p. 888.
21. *Freud on War, Sex and Neurosis* (New York: Arts and Science Press; 1947), p. 258.
22. Hermann Schmidt: "Die Entwicklung der Technik als Phase der Wandlung des Menschen," *Ztschr*. VDI, Bd. 96, Nr. 5.
23. Siegfried Aufhäuser: *An der Schwelle des Zeitalters der Angestellten* (Berlin-Wilmersdorf; 1963), p. 115.
24. Ludwig Neundörfer: *Die Angestellten: Neuer Versuch einer Standortbestimmung* (Stuttgart; 1961), p. 16.
25. Fritz Croner: *Soziologie der Angestellten* (Cologne, Berlin; 1962), p. 271.
26. Otto Stammer, ed.: *Angestellte und Arbeiter in der Betriebspyramide* (Berlin; 1959), p. 113.
27. Siegfried Braun: *Zur Soziologie der Angestellten* (Frankfurt am Main; 1964), p. 113.
28. Weber: *Economy and Society*, pp. 1402–3.
29. Margaret Mead: *Male and Female* (New York: Dell; 1949), p. 168.
30. Werner Correll: *Pädagogische Verhaltenspsychologie* (Munich-Basel; 1965), p. 23.
31. Alexander Mitscherlich: *Auf dem Weg zur vaterlosen Gesellschaft* (Munich; 1965), p. 27.
32. Konrad Lorenz: *On Aggression* (New York: Harcourt, Brace and World; 1966), p. 50.
33. Ibid., p. 271.
34. Figures from *Der Spiegel*, 45 (1967), p. 164.

Chapter 4

1. Theodor Eschenburg: *Über Autorität* (Frankfurt am Main; 1965), p. 9.
2. Karl Marx and Friedrich Engels: *Gesamtausgabe*, I, 536.
3. Elton Mayo: *The Human Problems of an Industrial Civilization* (New York: Viking Press; 1960).
4. Immanuel Kant: "Was ist Aufklärung?", *Berliner Monatschrift*, 1784.

INDEX

absurdist rebellion, 27, 41, 46, 85, 94, 157

activism, 25, 31, 140, 155, 159, 160, 166; and aggression, with frustration as connecting link between, 162; surplus, problem of, 167–8; *see also* aggression

"affluent criminality," 164

aggression, 24, 26, 32, 35, 111, 138–9, 159–64, 166; in youth movement, 44–5; in sexual behavior, 59–60, 61, 62, 64, 66, 71; and male role, 111, 112, 113; turned against itself, 132; intraspecific, 158; "pacific," 159; instigated by Communists, 160–1; political, 161, 166; and activism, with frustration as connecting link between, 162; surplus, problem of, 167–8; control of, 168; and universal self-enlightenment, 168–9; *see also* activism

alcohol, 88, 89

alienation, 30, 54

anarchism, 31, 38

anger, 24, 25, 27, 35, 41; literature of, 27–31; during sports events as hostility rituals, 34

Antiworlds (Voznesensky), 28 *n.*

art: kinetic, 41; pop, 41; erotic, 48

asceticism, 36, 38, 55

atom bomb, 116, 117, 118, 131

atomic stalemate, 121, 125, 126

Aufhäuser, Siegfried, quoted, 147

Augstein, Rudolf, quoted, 130–1

authoritarian state, 174, 176, 177

authority, 171–88 *passim;* military, changes in, 127, 128; defined, 173, 175; conscience as, 174; and democracy, 176, 183; and bureaucracy, 176–7, 183; need of broad distribution of, 184, 188

autism, in new sexual morality, 95

automation, 7, 25, 141

iii

A NOTE ABOUT THE AUTHOR

Karl Bednarik was born in Vienna, Austria, in 1915, where he still makes his home with his family. Educated at the Academy of Fine Arts in Vienna, he has been a painter, novelist, and script writer, before publishing a number of widely discussed sociological studies on such subjects as the new kind of blue-collar man, the consumer society, the rise of the programmers, and the youth cult of adaptability where the older generation stressed character. *The Male in Crisis* is his first book to be translated for publication in New York and London.

A NOTE ON THE TYPE

The text of this book was set on the Linotype in Janson, a recutting made direct from type cast from matrices long thought to have been made by the Dutchman Anton Janson, who was a practicing type founder in Leipzig during the years 1668–87. However, it has been conclusively demonstrated that these types are actually the work of Nicholas Kis (1650–1702), a Hungarian, who most probably learned his trade from the master Dutch type founder Kirk Voskens. The type is an excellent example of the influential and sturdy Dutch types that prevailed in England up to the time William Caslon developed his own incomparable designs from these Dutch faces.

This book was composed, printed, and bound by
The Book Press, Brattleboro, Vermont

Typography and binding design by
RICHARD–GABRIEL RUMMONDS